The Room With The Garden View

Ben Nelson

The Room with the Garden View

By Ben Nelson

The Room with the Garden View

Published by Ben Nelson

Dedicated to my incredible wife, Cassidy, and to our kids, Kye and Wendy, who fill our home with joy, laughter, and purpose. And to my Collectivus Church family, thank you for living this message with me, not just reading it.

Introduction

In 2009, I embarked on a honeymoon adventure to Jamaica with my wife, Cassidy. We were young, in love, and most of all, broke. She had just graduated with her master's degree but was burdened with student debt. I was a youth pastor and worship pastor, and my paycheck reflected the reality of the job. I had saved for months to pay for this honeymoon, and moments before leaving, we received a promotional email stating that we had qualified for an upgrade to "a room with a garden view" for only $35 more a night. After checking my nearly empty bank account, we decided to pull the trigger and get the upgrade.

As we settled into our room, we were amazed at its beauty and well-designed amenities. However, what truly set it apart was the incredible view of the garden. Every day, we marveled at its beauty and couldn't take our eyes off it. We found ourselves so captivated by the view that we rarely left our room, content to simply gaze at the splendor before us.

But one day, while taking in the view, I noticed something peculiar. A young couple was strolling through the garden. I turned to my bride and said, "Who do they think they are strolling through our garden?" I was irritated that they were enjoying its beauty without an upgraded room like ours. It was then that Cassidy brought to my attention that the garden was for everyone to enjoy, and we didn't have to settle for merely observing it from a distance.

Unfortunately, too often, the Christian faith has become a place where we settle for a room with a garden view. We attend church services, participate in small groups, and volunteer in ministries, but we do not truly experience the fullness of God's kingdom. We become content with observing the beauty of the garden from a distance rather than entering it and experiencing it for ourselves. We, as believers, have settled for a room with a garden view. We build churches and communities, but we rarely experience the fullness of God's kingdom.

The truth is, Jesus came to offer us a way back to the garden, back to God's initial intent in Eden. Our churches, faith communities, and personal faith have built a space for you to observe the Kingdom of God from afar, even though Jesus came to lead us back to the Garden and to God's original intent in Eden. The church has done an impressive job of creating an all-inclusive resort that provides a glimpse of the garden, but the gardener has personally invited us inside. This invitation is not just to witness His goodness from a distance, but to experience it up close and personal. We can truly encounter the garden for ourselves! Our invitation is not just a front-row seat to the garden, but an opportunity to experience its fullness and wonder firsthand. God's invitation is not just to observe His goodness from afar, but to embrace it intimately. He doesn't want us to settle for a faith that only allows us to observe from a distance. He wants us to experience it up close, to taste and see the goodness of the Lord for ourselves (Psalm 34:8). We don't have to settle for a false narrative that guides us down a path of mediocrity. Instead, we can embrace the real truth and experience the abundant life that God has prepared for us (John 10:10).

The Garden of Eden reveals God's initial intent for our lives. It was a place of perfect communion with Him, a place where humanity walked in perfect harmony with their Creator. But sin entered the world, and we were separated from God. However, through Jesus Christ, we can be reconciled to God and experience His original intent for our lives. We can enter the garden, experience its fullness, and walk in perfect harmony with our Creator.

Friend, it's time to experience life in the garden for yourself. It's time to move beyond the room with a garden view and into the fullness of God's kingdom. It's time to embrace the real truth and live the abundant life that Jesus has prepared for you.

Section One: Deemed

Before there was sin, shame, or separation, there was God's declaration over humanity. Man and woman were created in His image, placed in the Garden, and entrusted with His creation. To understand what Jesus came to redeem, we must first understand what God deemed.

Chapter One: God's Initial Intent

God's initial intent is His final decision. This statement begs the question, what exactly was God's initial intent? What was the plan when He first created man and woman and placed them in the Garden of Eden?

Understanding God's initial intent helps us comprehend His ultimate goal. While we, as believers, readily accept Jesus' redemption story without comprehending God's initial intent for the world, it's difficult to grasp the fullness of that redemption. How can the world be redeemed without knowing what it was first "deemed"? For too long, we have misinterpreted God's initial intent and the Garden of Eden's true significance. This lack of truth is leading us to embrace or fabricate a false narrative. You see, when we don't know the truth, any story can become our narrative. I believe that it is time to shift our perspective and gain a clearer understanding of God's true intentions.

As we gain a deeper understanding of God's initial intent, we can appreciate the magnitude of the "fall" and the lengths to which Jesus went to redeem us all. It is only by knowing God's initial intent that we can fully understand how far the world has deviated from it. The garden in which God placed humanity was meant to be a place of harmony, but sin entered the world, disrupting that harmony and unity. However,

God never wavered from His original plan, and through Jesus, He has made a way for all people to be reconciled to Him.

My desire is for each of us to gain a proper perspective on God's initial intent for our lives and humanity. To achieve this, we must also recognize that our understanding is limited. We see only a small piece of the puzzle, while God sees the whole picture. However, I believe that as we study the Scriptures and seek God's guidance, we will begin to see His initial intent and the path back to it. I implore you to trust in His wisdom and goodness, knowing that God always has the best interests of His sons and daughters at heart.

Over the next 11 chapters, I hope to remind you that God's initial intent is His final decision. As we seek to live according to His initial intent, we can experience the same kind of unity and peace that was present in the garden. Though sin still exists in the world, we can find hope in the fact that God's ultimate purpose will one day be fulfilled and that His Kingdom is at hand.

Though God eagerly desires for you and me to embrace redemption fully, it is evident that our enemy, Satan, is always seeking to deceive believers by leading them to buy into false narratives and lies. One of his most used tactics is to distort and pervert the truth about God's plan and intention for humanity. In doing so, the enemy causes us to settle for less than what God initially intended. This type of deception is dangerous! It is dangerous because it blinds us to the true nature of God and His intent for His children. As we allow false narratives to shape our understanding of God and faith, we miss out on the transformative power of the truth. What lies have we embraced as truths?

The Bible warns us repeatedly about the danger of being deceived. In the gospel of Matthew, Jesus says,

Matthew 24:24
"For false messiahs and false prophets will appear and perform great signs and wonders to deceive, if possible, even the elect."

The Apostle Paul also urges believers to be on guard against deception, warning that Satan disguises himself as an angel of light (2 Corinthians 11:14). Scripture reveals that the only way to avoid deception is to cling to the truth. But how do we cling to the truth when we are holding on to lies?

God's initial intent was for us to experience the culture of heaven on earth. The Kingdom of God, in its purest form, is the garden as described in Genesis 1 and 2. I pray the following chapters offer a blueprint for God's initial intent, showing us the kind of world God intended for us to live in. Every detail was intentional, and there was no element of chance or accident.

To understand what we were first “deemed,” let's return to the very beginning. As we journey through the creation story, let me first clarify that this book is not a debate on whether the creation story is a literal seven days or a narrative meant to illustrate and reveal the process of God’s intentional design. Rather, it is an opportunity to reveal and display God’s heart and desire for His children. I believe that only by studying His Word and allowing the Holy Spirit to guide us can we gain a clear insight and understanding of God's plan for our lives. In the gospel of John, Jesus says,

John 8:32
"Then you will know the truth, and the truth will set you free."

When we embrace the truth about God and His ways, we are set free from the bondage of false narratives and deception. We will only embrace the truth when we are willing to change our minds and hearts as God reveals truths we have missed along the way.

At Collectivus Church, we pray a variation of the same prayer every week before the message. The prayer goes something like this:

'God, give us ears that can hear, a mind that is open, and a heart that is willing. Ears that are inclined to You and not to the things striving for our attention. A mind that is open and willing to set aside any preconceived ideas of who You are, or any false narratives we may have embraced or fabricated along the way, that stand in the way of Your truth. And a heart that is willing to respond in obedience. Amen.'

I then ask, *'Today, are you willing to change your mind?'* Not *'Today, you must change your mind,'* but *'Are you willing to change your mind?'* Meaning, if we gain new knowledge and truth from God, would we be willing to think differently? That is the posture we must have when approaching the subject of God's initial and final intent for our lives as well.

In the beginning, it is revealed that God created the world with a specific purpose and intentionality. He showed us how life could be when everything was ideal and aligned with His initial intent. When God created "the heavens and the earth," it was not meant to be a contrasting statement, but rather a phrase that showed two complementary elements. In the Garden of Eden, we see a perfect and ideal setting in which everything was very good and created for the benefit of all involved. The Garden, Earth, was not intended to stand in contrast to heaven but rather to complement it in intentional Kingdom rhythms.

However, we have embraced the lie that heaven and earth are opposing ideas instead of their initial design. Because of the false narrative propagated by Satan, the gap between Earth and Heaven has become far too wide. Satan has corrupted our view of who God is and what He intended to do through His Son, Jesus, the one who brings redemption to the world. Jesus, the one who came so that we could commune with God unhindered by our sins once again.

1 Corinthians 15:55-57

"Where, O death, is your victory? Where, O death, is your sting?" 56
The sting of death is sin, and the power of sin is the law. 57 But thanks

be to God! He gives us the victory through our Lord Jesus Christ.

We, as believers, have reduced Jesus' mission to, "Jesus died for sins so that we could one day get into Heaven." While this is one of the most important truths we will ever receive, it is still only part of the truth. And when a partial truth becomes the whole story, it can quietly become a believable lie.

Here is the full Truth: God is calling us back to the Garden, which is His initial intent for humanity. God's initial intent is made clear in Genesis 1 and 2. This is where we find the ideal blueprint for God's original plan. In the Garden, humanity walked in perfect harmony with God and enjoyed the fullness of His provision. It was a place where the Kingdom of Heaven was fully received on Earth.

Through the death and resurrection of Jesus, God made a way for us to be reconciled to Him and to experience the fullness of His Kingdom once again. Jesus' mission was not just to secure our place in Heaven, but to restore us to the original intent God had for us in the Garden. This is why Jesus taught us to pray,

Matthew 6:10

"Your Kingdom come, Your will be done, on Earth as it is in Heaven"

God's desire is for us to embrace the Kingdom that is at hand and thrive, not just survive until one day we get to heaven. He longs for us to experience the culture of Heaven on Earth, to live within His presence, and to experience the blessing of embracing the garden. This culture of Heaven is referred to as "The Kingdom." The Kingdom of God is the culture of Heaven here on Earth. As believers, we need to reject the false narratives that have distorted our view of God and embrace the truth of His original intent for humanity. When we view God incorrectly, we stand at a distance and create churches and religious practices that only see the Kingdom through a peephole, a room with a garden view, if you will. But when we embrace the truth, we will experience the abundant life that Jesus promised. This comes once we fully grasp our identity and purpose in accordance with God's initial intent.

Before we can fully grasp our true identity and purpose, we must first understand an essential principle: *God's presence preceded our presence.* God prepared a place for us before He even formed us. This means that our existence is not a random accident or a mistake, but a deliberate act of God's love and grace. Our lives are not meaningless or purposeless, but rather part of God's greater story of redemption and restoration. Because of this, we can have confidence that we were created with intention and purpose, and that God's initial intent is also His final decision. This does not mean that we haven't taken detours along the way, but it does mean that we have a God who knows us, loves us, and is for us. We can trust in His goodness and faithfulness as we seek to discover and fulfill our unique calling in His Kingdom. Every place you go, He has gone before you. God didn't just drop you into this random place in the cosmos and wish you luck. One of the greatest truths about creation is that God's *presence precedes all things.*

Genesis 1:1
"In the beginning, God created the heavens and the earth."

God was present before the creation of the world, and He knew exactly what He was creating. He designed everything with intentionality, knowing that each piece would play a unique role in the bigger picture. As children of God, we can find comfort in the fact that God knew us before we were even born. We see when God speaks to Jeremiah:

Jeremiah 1:5

"Before I formed you in the womb I knew you, before you were born, I set you apart; I appointed you as a prophet to the nations."

This truth was not isolated to Jeremiah; the same truth applies to us. God created us with great intentionality, and He has a plan for our lives. We are not accidents or afterthoughts. We are God's masterpiece, created with intention and purpose.

We are unique in persons yet united in purpose.

It's important to remember that when life seems chaotic and messy, it doesn't mean God is absent. He is always present, and His presence is what gives us hope and peace. Even when we can't see the bigger picture, we can trust that God is working all things together for our good. As Paul says to the church in Rome,

Romans 8:28

"And we know that in all things God works for the good of those who love him, who have been called according to his purpose."

My prayer today is that this book will help you take comfort in the fact that God knew us before we were even born and created us with intentionality and divine nature. I pray you embrace the fact that He is the one who “deemed” you in the beginning. He is the great artist who prepared the canvas on which His greatest masterpiece would reside. We can trust that His presence goes before us, and He is always working for our good. Despite our fallen nature being tainted by sin, we must remember that goodness is our deemed nature, as we were created in the image of a good and perfect God. We are invited to participate in the divine nature of our Father, not just the fallen nature of our flesh.

God's goodness is evident in all that He created, as seen in Genesis 1:25, where it says that *"God saw that it was good"* when He made the wild animals, livestock, and creatures that move along the ground. Everything God created was good. This goodness is not just limited to the physical creation, but also extends to the gifts God gives us.

We must begin to understand that when we trust God, we can be assured that He will never give us something bad. This is faith. *Faith is when our hope in God is embraced as truth instead of wishful thinking.* The reason we place our hope in God, trust in His promises, and embrace His Word as truth instead of wishful thinking is because God is, and has always been, faithful and good. It goes against His nature to give something bad to His children. This does not mean that life will always be good. This does not mean that bad things will not happen. The truth is, if it isn't good, then it isn't from God. That truth does not cancel out your grief or your pain. It simply means that a good God never stops being good, even when life does not feel that way. This does not mean every painful thing comes from outside God's sovereign hand. It means His character behind every circumstance remains untainted, even when the circumstance itself is not.

The idea of God giving bad gifts stands in opposition to His redemption story and to His promise to be a "Good Father." However, we may not always understand the gifts that God gives us, or we may not be in the correct position to see the truth behind His giving. In these situations, we need to trust that God is good and that ultimately everything He gives us is for our good. God has always been faithful, and His goodness has always existed. *His faithfulness does not stop with your story or situation.*

In our faith journey with God, we may feel anxious or sometimes worried about what He might ask us to do. We may even be afraid that God will ask us to do something that we don't want to do. But if we truly understand the heart of a good God, we will know that God always has our best interests at heart. You may not always understand His ways, but you can trust them. *Knowing God is what leads us to trusting God.* Believing He is a good Father is key to receiving the things He is offering. God's plans for us are always good, and His desire is for us to thrive and not just merely survive.

I remember when I was 19 years old, I worked at a barbecue joint. Late one evening, while we were getting ready to close, I was taking out the trash. I asked a friend to give me the keys so I could come back inside the back door. Well, he did give them to me. In fact, he actually threw the keys hard. But with bags of trash in both hands, I couldn't catch what he was throwing me. In fact, the keys hit me in the chest. I shouted at him, *"Why would you throw me the keys while my hands were full?"* He promptly replied, *"Was the trash so important that you couldn't drop it to catch the keys?"* We laughed, but the real question remained. Why did I hold onto the trash instead of catching the keys?

Often, we miss what God is trying to give because we'd much rather hold onto the trash we're carrying. What is so important that we cannot let it go to receive what He has for us? If you desire to live a life that reflects God's redeeming work, one that is different from your current reality, it may be time to let go of the trash. James, Jesus' brother, reminds us of this in His letter to the church:

James 1:17
Every good and perfect gift is from above, coming down from the Father of the heavenly lights, who does not change like shifting shadows.

We worry about the things God might ask us to do, stress about what it means to truly follow Him, and worry, *"What if God asks me to do something I don't want to do?"* But if we find ourselves in this position, it simply means we don't fully understand the heart of a truly good and redeeming God.

On this journey with God, we need to learn to let go of the "trash" that we are carrying and be willing to receive the good gifts that God wants to give us. If we hold on to the things that weigh us down, we may miss out on the good things God has in store for us. So let us trust in the goodness of God, and let go of anything that hinders us from receiving His good gifts. When we trust in Him, we will see that He has always gone before us, and everything He has created has been according to His divine design.

In the Gospel of John, we see the story of Jesus resurrecting His friend Lazarus from the dead.

John 11:41-44
" 41 So they took away the stone. Then Jesus looked up and said, "Father, I thank you that you have heard me. 42 I knew that you always hear me, but I said this for the benefit of the people standing here, that they may believe that you sent me." 43 When he had said this, Jesus called in a loud voice, "Lazarus, come out!" 44 The dead man came out, his hands and feet wrapped with strips of linen, and a cloth around his face. Jesus said to them, "Take off the grave clothes and let him go."

Remember, God's desire for us since the fall of man has been for us to be redeemed to what we were first *"deemed"* to be. In the beginning, God declared all that He created as *"good."* But as sin entered the world, we became burdened with old, smelly grave clothes, holding onto things that identify us with death. Yet, God longs to give us something much, much better, something that will lead us to true life. A life in communion with God and in alignment with His initial design. We have settled in viewing the garden instead of returning to it. Laying down our ways for His ways. Just as Jesus commanded Lazarus to remove his grave clothes, God's desire for us is to remove the old, to let go of the things that weigh us down and keep us bound to the past. Jesus' purpose was not merely to transform the immoral into moral individuals, but to resurrect those who were spiritually dead into newness of life. He didn't come to make bad people good people, He came to make dead things come to life again! *He came to invite you back to the garden.*

Allow me to offer you a plot twist that maybe you've never considered before. *Lazarus didn't have any other clothes to wear!* Jesus was asking him to remove the only clothing he had. Hear me clearly. God calls us out of the old life, the old ways of thinking, and the old ways of doing things. He calls us to shed our old ways and put on the new life that He has prepared for us. However, we often hold on to the past, thinking that it's all we have. Just as Lazarus did not have any other clothes to wear, we may fear we will have nothing left if we give our old ways to God. This is where our faith must come into play. Remember how we defined faith before? *Faith is when our hope in God is embraced as truth instead of wishful thinking.* We must trust that God's ways are higher than our ways, and that His plans for us are good.

We may fear that if we follow God, our relationships will change, our career paths will shift, or we will have to let go of the hurt inflicted upon us by others. This is a good possibility. But we must remember that trusting God is not a byproduct of knowing what God knows, but rather a byproduct of trusting that God knows. The garden is open, but we are afraid to leave the well-beaten paths of this world in order to embrace a path that leads to the garden.

Today, can we take off our old grave clothes and put on something new? Let's step away from our room that has only a view of the garden, knowing we can walk in it once again! Let us trust in the goodness of God and have faith that He will give us something much better. Let us remember that *God's initial intent is His final decision*, and that everything that comes from God is good. In the beginning, God created everything good, and He longs to restore us to that original state of goodness. He wants to redeem us and make us new, but we must be willing to let go of the past and trust in Him fully.

Knowing what we are first deemed is essential to our redemption. We cannot fully grasp the extent of God's love and the redemption He has for us without understanding that we were first created in His image, and that His original intent for us was good. We must also understand that God's initial intent is His final decision, and He is always working towards restoring us to that original design.

That story of Lazarus serves as a powerful analogy for our own journey of redemption. Just as Lazarus was raised from the dead, we too can experience new life in Christ. However, like Lazarus, we may still be wearing our old, smelly grave clothes. We hold onto the things that identify us with death, rather than embracing the new life that Christ has for us. But God wants to give us something far greater. He wants to give us the abundant life that He intended for us from the very beginning. He wants to walk with us in the garden once again.

We must let go of the things that hold us back and trust that God knows what is best for us. We must believe that his initial intent for us was good, and that He has a plan to redeem us to that original design. This requires faith and trust in God's character, knowing that He is a good and loving Father who desires the best for us.

Remember what we were first deemed when created in God's image, and that He has a plan to redeem us to that original design. We must let go of the things that hold us back and trust that God knows what is best for us. We must believe that His initial intent for us was good, and that He has a plan to bring about our redemption. With faith and trust in God's character, we can experience the fullness of the abundant life He has for us. Why? Because God’s initial intent is His final decision!

Chapter Two: Our Original Identity

A few years back, I wrote about the significance of seeing God clearly in my book, *Proper Perspective.* We often see ourselves in unhealthy and incorrect ways because of our distorted and unhealthy view of God. When we perceive God correctly, we can see ourselves, God, and life more accurately. Knowing the truth about God and understanding his heart help us comprehend our true selves. Knowing God can reveal a lot more about children than we ever thought possible.

But who are you, really? Who are you in the eyes of God? Not who the world has made you to be, or the circumstances that molded you. It's essential to grasp our true identity in God's eyes in order to return to the garden. *God created you, but the world is corrupting you.* I want to make something clear, so there is no confusion or misunderstanding: when we use terms like *'corrupt'* or *'perverted,'* our minds can sometimes jump to extreme ideas. Rather, it suggests that something has become a lesser version of itself or has lost its true identity. Unfortunately, many of the lies we believe about ourselves revolve around our identity. The world corrupts and distorts our identity with some of the most significant lies we've ever been told. Genesis 1 explains that God created things according to their kind. However, God created you, not according to your kind, but according to His kind. Let's discover the truth about our identity in God and dive deeper into who we really are.

In Genesis 1, we see that God created everything according to "their kind." He starts with inanimate objects like light, water, and vegetation. Look what happens when He creates vegetation:

Genesis 1:11

Then God said, "Let the land produce vegetation: seed-bearing plants and trees on the land that bear fruit with seed in it, according to their various kinds." And it was so.

Do you see this? He created all those things according to "their kind," then He shifts to "creatures":

Genesis 1:20-21

And God said, "Let the water teem with living creatures, and let birds fly above the earth across the vault of the sky." So God created the great creatures of the sea and every living thing with which the water teems and that moves about in it, according to their kinds, and every winged bird according to its kind. And God saw that it was good.

Genesis 1:24

And God said, "Let the land produce living creatures according to their kinds: the livestock, the creatures that move along the ground, and the wild animals, each according to its kind." And it was so.

How did He create animals? According to what? He created each according to "its kind." But when it came to human beings, He created us differently. Let's read together.

Genesis 1:26-31

"Then God said, 'Let us make mankind in our image, in our likeness, so that they may rule over the fish in the sea and the birds in the sky, over the livestock and all the wild animals, and over all the creatures that move along the ground.' So God created mankind in his own image, in the image of God he created them; male and female he created them. God blessed them and said to them, 'Be fruitful and increase in number; fill the earth and subdue it. Rule over the fish in the sea and the birds in the sky and over every living creature that moves on the ground.' Then God said, 'I give you every seed-bearing plant on the face of the whole earth and every tree that has fruit with seed in it. They will be yours for food. And to all the beasts of the earth and all the birds in the sky and all the creatures that move along the ground—everything that has the

breath of life in it—I give every green plant for food.' And it was so. God saw all that he had made, and it was very good. And there was evening, and there was morning—the sixth day."

Do you see it? This is incredible! God created everything in the world according to "its kind," from the animals to the plants, but when it came to us, He created us according to "His kind." This distinction is crucial because it highlights that we are not like anything else in the world. We are uniquely crafted by God to reflect His image, character, and nature.

So, if God created us according to His kind, why are we allowing people to define us according to their kind?

It is easy to fall into the trap of comparing ourselves to others since that's what we see around us. However, we must understand that we were not created to be like everyone else. Comparing ourselves to others only leads to dissatisfaction and a loss of purpose. Instead, we should focus on comparing ourselves to the person God first "deemed" us to be. We should care about what the one who created us, according to "His kind," thinks.

We must strive to discover and live out our true identity in Christ, as He is the only one who can reveal it to us. When we stop comparing ourselves to others and focus on our unique identity in Christ, we can truly live a fulfilled life that brings glory to God. Our true identity is not based on what the world has made us into, but on who God created us to be in the beginning. Satan loves to corrupt the way we see ourselves by telling us lies about our identity. He blurs our vision and causes us to doubt our true identity in God.

It is important to know our true identity because our design determines how we interact with God, the Kingdom, and the entire world around us. When we see ourselves as God sees us, we can fulfill the purpose He has for us and live our lives to the fullest. We can embrace His desire to walk with us in the garden once again. Our identity in Christ is the foundation of our faith and the key to our future.

Knowing who we are in God's eyes is a critical step towards getting back to the garden. We must understand that our true identity is based on who God created us to be, not on the lies that Satan tries to tell us. When we see ourselves clearly, we can see God more clearly, and vice versa. Our relationship with God is strengthened when we know our true identity, enabling us to fulfill our purpose in the Kingdom.

Understanding our identity is crucial to living a fulfilling life in Christ. We were created in God's image and likeness, and our design determines how we interact with the world around us. Satan tries to corrupt our identity by telling us lies, but we must reject those lies and hold onto the truth of who we are in Christ. We are children of God, and by stepping into this identity, we can fulfill our purpose in the Kingdom and live the life God intended for us.

Looking back at the account of creation, we discover that God created everything according to its kind, but when it came to creating human beings, He created us in his image and likeness. This concept of *Imago Dei* - the image of God - is a foundational truth that speaks to our very identity and purpose in life.

We were created to reflect God's nature and character and to have a unique relationship with Him that sets us apart from the rest of creation. As the Psalmist reminds us in the 8th chapter of Psalms:

Psalm 8:4-5
"What is man that you are mindful of him, and the son of man that you care for him? Yet you have made him a little lower than the heavenly

beings and crowned him with glory and honor."

We must begin to embrace that our true identity is not based on our circumstances, our past mistakes, or even our current behavior. Our identity is rooted in the fact that we are made in the image and likeness of God. This is not just a spiritual or philosophical concept but a tangible reality that shapes how we view ourselves and interact with the world around us. When we embrace our identity as God's masterpiece, we can begin to see ourselves in a whole new light. We are not just random beings existing on this earth; we are unique creations with the identity of children of God. As the Apostle Paul reminds us in his letter to the church of Ephesus:

Ephesians 2:10
"For we are his workmanship, created in Christ Jesus for good works, which God prepared beforehand, that we should walk in them."

You may be interested to know that, before pursuing Biblical studies, I was an art major in college. Even to this day, I continue to appreciate art and its impact on our lives. During my time as an art major, I learned that the term *"masterpiece"* is not based solely on its beauty or skillful execution, nor even on the artist's name. Rather, a work is designated a masterpiece because of its unique and individual qualities. Such works are considered priceless because there is nothing else in the world that is exactly like it. In fact, copies of masterpieces cannot compare to the original and are not as valuable.

In the same way that a masterpiece of art finds much of its value in its uniqueness and individuality, we, too, are priceless because there is no one else in the world exactly like us. Stop trying to be imitations or copies of others. *Many of the individuals you are envious of don't even share your value*s. You are attempting to imitate and emulate people whose lives are not guided by the same principles as yours. We were created with a specific set of talents, gifts, and abilities that are meant to be used for God's glory and to impact the world around us. It's time to regain proper perspective and see yourself the way God sees you, as His greatest masterpiece, made in His image and likeness. We are unique in persons yet united in purpose. Satan tries to define you by your mistakes and sins, but may we never forget that *our true identity is rooted in our design, not in our departure.*

Again, the concept of our true identity being in the image and likeness of God is not new. It is rooted in the very beginning of creation. It is rooted in the creation story.

Genesis 1:27
"So God created man in His own image; in the image of God He created him; male and female He created them"

This means that every single human being on this planet was created in the image of God, and therefore, we all have inherent worth and value. *All people have sacred value*

However, as I mentioned, Satan loves to twist the truth and lead us astray. He knows that if he can convince us to base our identity on fleeting and temporary things, then we will never fully understand our true worth and purpose. That's why it's so important for us to recognize and remember our true identity in God.

Growing up, I would spend hours with my pencils and paper, bringing my imagination to life on the page. One day, I decided to try my hand at drawing a portrait of my dad. I studied his face, taking note of every detail, and began to sketch. As I worked, I realized that creating a portrait was different from creating something from my own imagination. I couldn't just make up features or take shortcuts. I had to pay close attention to the original and replicate it as accurately as possible. I couldn't create my dad in my own image or make him look like something else entirely. I had to create him according to his kind, his original identity.

In the same way, we were created in the image of God. We are not free to create ourselves in our own image or make ourselves into something we're not. We must pay close attention to our initial design and begin to replicate it as accurately as possible. We were created according to His kind, not according to our kind. We can't change who God created us to be, but we can embrace our original identity and live out the life for which we were created. Likewise, we cannot begin to create God in "our image," because in doing so, we allow earthly traits to leak into our image of a perfect heavenly Father.

The Psalmist tells us that we are “fearfully and wonderfully made” (Psalm 139:14). This means that God intentionally created us in a unique and beautiful way, just as an artist creates a masterpiece. And like a masterpiece, each one of us is priceless and irreplaceable. We were not created to be copies of someone else or to blend in with the world around us. Instead, we were created to shine our own unique light in this world and reflect the glory of God. *Unique in persons yet united in purpose.*

It's time to let go of the false identities that the world tries to impose on us and embrace our true identity in God. When we embrace false narratives about our identity, we neglect to participate in the Kingdom and begin to view the garden from a distance, instead of participating in the divine nature in which God created us. As we do so, we will discover our true life and be able to fulfill the Great Commission of representing God on earth. Let us strive to view ourselves and others through the lens of the image and likeness of God, recognizing the divine nature within each and every one of us.

For far too long, you've allowed the world to define you and give you a sense of self-worth and value. You've looked to your accomplishments, possessions, social status, and relationships to determine your identity. But the truth is, your identity is not found in any of those things. *Your true identity is found in the image and likeness of God.*

When God created you, He created you in His image and likeness. This means that you have all of His unique qualities and characteristics. You are one-of-a-kind, and there is no one like you on planet Earth. You are His greatest masterpiece, and He has deemed you to be priceless. This is why you must start seeing yourself the way God sees you.

Satan, our enemy, wants nothing more than to blur your perspective and keep you from realizing your true identity in God. He wants you to believe the lies that the world tells you about who you are, but you must resist those lies and embrace the truth about your identity in God.

It's time to start viewing yourself in a different way than ever before. It's time to shed the false narratives that you've believed about yourself and embrace the truth that you are a child of God, created in His image and likeness. To return to the Garden, it is essential to rediscover your true identity and acknowledge your divine nature. When you do this, you will begin to see yourself in a new light and be able to live the life that God has for you. Your purpose is to reflect God's image on Earth. However, to represent God, you must first grasp and recollect how God revealed Himself. *In other words, your true identity, the essence of who you are, is entirely based on God's truth.*

Remember, the story of Creation teaches us that God created us in His image and likeness. Our true identity is found in Him, and we must resist the lies that the world tells us about who we are. This should also shape how we view others. Satan would love for you to think that other people are your enemy, but that is all a distraction that removes you from seeing Satan as the true enemy and others as your brothers and sisters in Christ. We are God's crowning achievement, His greatest masterpiece. When we start seeing ourselves the way God sees us, we will be able to fulfill the purpose He has for our lives and experience the perfection and beauty of the garden He has called us back to.

Chapter Three: The Forbidden Fruit

With knowledge comes responsibility. This principle was first revealed through the story of the Garden of Eden when Adam and Eve tasted the forbidden fruit and, in doing so, changed the course of human history forever. In a single moment, everything seemed to go terribly wrong. But what was it about the fruit of the tree of knowledge that made it forbidden?

Growing up, my mother said I would argue with a signpost, that I would argue for argument's sake. And there may be some truth to that, but honestly, I just wanted answers. I was tired of people withholding information from me because of my age or maturity. I always thought there was information that could give me answers that adults had chosen to safeguard, and I could not understand why.

The question, "What was the fruit that Adam and Eve ate?" was one of those questions. I figured one day I would be told an answer. The years went and still no answer. Maybe it wasn't because they didn't want to tell me, but because no one in my life had an answer. So, I kept asking: "What was the forbidden fruit? Why did God not want them to experience the things that came with it?"

Again, these are the questions I had as a young child. These questions were often answered with a combative tone that seemed to shun me for "questioning God." What I learned is that our questions will not break God. They may offend your pastor, stump your Sunday school teacher, or possibly break the Western church, but they will not break God. God loves our questions.

So, what was it about the fruit of the tree of knowledge that made it forbidden? Beyond its common use as a simple story of disobedience and the origin of sin, the account of Adam and Eve, whether you read it as a historical account, a theological narrative, or a symbolic story carrying moral truth, speaks to a deeper truth that we often miss, a present-day reality that remains hidden in plain sight.

The Bible tells us that the fruit came from "the tree of the knowledge of good and evil." So, the fruit of this tree was the "knowledge of good and evil." Just as an apple tree produces apples, the name of the tree reveals the fruit it bears. So why did God not want them to have the knowledge of good and evil? Because there is a burden that comes with that fruit.

Herein lies the problem: with knowledge of good and evil comes the responsibility to determining what is good and what is bad. *Judgment of good and evil is the burden.* This seat of judgment is one that God never intended for us to have and one that Adam and Eve were not equipped to handle at that time. God had created them to live in perfect harmony with Him and each other, without the burden of navigating the complexities of morality and ethics. However, by eating the fruit, they took on a responsibility that they were not prepared for, and their perfect world began to crumble. This is a burdensome weight that we cannot escape. God's desire was for us to be reliant on Him to be the Judge. *In an attempt to take on the seat of Judge, we found ourselves in the judgment seat.*

In the beginning, Adam and Eve were childlike in their trust for the Creator and were not burdened with the responsibility of judging good and evil. However, with the knowledge of good and evil, they now had to face the consequences of their actions and be held accountable for their choices. We once were ignorant, and you can't hold ignorance accountable. *Information invites accountability.*

As we examine this truth in scripture, we begin to realize that maybe ignorance truly was bliss. The burden of being responsible for their own actions was too much for Adam and Eve to bear, and they lost their childlike innocence. This serves as a warning for us, as we also carry the weight of the knowledge of good and evil, and we must be careful not to become burdened with the responsibility of judging others. We must strive to maintain our childlike trust in the Creator and resist the temptation to take on more than we were meant to bear.

By eating the fruit, Adam and Eve took on a responsibility that was never meant for them, and they became judges and bad judges at that. Adam and Eve were bad judges, and that should indicate that we are as well.

Wait, why do we think they are bad judges? Here's why: before eating from the tree of the knowledge of good and evil, God had deemed everything "good." As we discussed in depth in Chapter 1, everything was as God initially intended. But when Adam and Eve took on the knowledge of good and evil, they instantly began labeling things "bad" in a world where everything had just been labeled "good." They looked at their bodies and labeled them "bad," then began to cover them. They heard God walking in the garden and began to hide, because that wonderful and perfect God could be "bad" if they had to make their own judgment call. The truth is, they became bad judges, unable to handle the burden of judgment that came with their newfound knowledge.

This begs the question: how much more do we misjudge things out of our inability to bear that burden? We live in a world that is divided and broken, a world where good and evil exist side by side, and we are constantly faced with the challenge of distinguishing between the two. Unlike the garden, our world is sin-fractured and broken. We may think we are good judges, but the truth is that our judgments are often clouded by our limited understanding and biased perspectives. We label things as "good" or "bad" based on our own experiences and opinions, without considering the broader context and the complexities of the situation. If Adam and Eve were able to misjudge good and evil in a purely good world, how much more likely are we to misjudge and mislabel things as good or evil?

I am not asking this question to make you question your moral code or the convictions of our faith. I am revealing this principle so that we can begin to walk with theological and moral humility. *We are bad judges.* This is not a call to moral passivity. It is an invitation to hold our verdicts loosely, extending to others the same grace we desperately need ourselves.

Moreover, our judgments are often driven by fear and insecurity. We often judge others to feel superior and validate our own beliefs and values, rather than seeking understanding and compassion. We misjudge others and ourselves, and in doing so, we perpetuate the cycle of pain and suffering that plagues our world. *We pursue knowledge more than we pursue truth.*

There is a difference between the discernment we are called to and the condemnation that belongs to God alone. We can and must evaluate truth, test doctrine, and distinguish good from evil, but we must hold our verdicts loosely and leave final condemnation in God's hands.

While it is clear that the knowledge of good and evil was a burden that we were never meant to carry, it is also important to remember that knowledge in itself is not inherently bad. In fact, knowledge is a gift God has given us to navigate the world around us and make informed decisions. What we need is a true understanding, a complete knowledge that aligns with God's truth. The problem arises when we buy into propaganda and misinformation fed to us by the world through an enemy whose primary goal is to deceive and mislead us.

When we took on the burden of judging, the enemy's main tactic became lies, infiltrating our thoughts and distorting the way we see God, ourselves, and others. In a world where misinformation and half-truths are rampant, it's easy to be led astray. However, as followers of Christ, we must align ourselves with the knowledge of Christ. We must pursue truth instead of simply accumulating knowledge. As Jesus said:

John 8:32
"You shall know the truth, and the truth shall make you free."

We must seek out God's truth and reject the enemy's lies. It's crucial to be discerning and wise, not only in what we believe but also in how we process information. We must test everything against God's truth, as Paul says in his letter to the church of the Thessalonians:

1 Thessalonians 5:21
"Test everything; hold on to what is good."

Are we in pursuit of knowledge or truth? We must be mindful of what we're pursuing and why. We must seek out knowledge that aligns with

God's truth and use it for His glory. As we do, we will grow in our understanding of who God is and who He has created us to be.

As human beings, our knowledge is limited and imperfect. We cannot fully comprehend the complexity of the universe, let alone the mind of God. That's why it's important to recognize that our understanding of things is always fallible. This is especially true when our knowledge comes into contradiction with God's Word and nature. When faced with such a contradiction, we must be humble enough to acknowledge the limitations of our own knowledge and understanding. We must remember that God's wisdom and knowledge are beyond our reach, and that our judgments will always fall short of the ultimate judge. But acknowledging the limitations of our own knowledge is not enough. We must also cultivate a deep sense of trust in God. We must be willing to lay down our own ways for His, to surrender our own limited understanding to His infinite wisdom.

In pursuing this trust, we must also recognize that there is a difference between knowledge and truth. Knowledge is merely a collection of facts and information, but truth is the realization of that knowledge. In other words, *truth is the application of knowledge in a way that aligns with the ultimate reality of God's nature and will.* Therefore, in pursuing truth, we must be willing to put aside our preconceptions and biases and to seek out the guidance of the Holy Spirit. We must be open to new perspectives and ideas, and willing to let go of our limited understanding to embrace the fullness of God's truth.

Trust is the answer when our limited knowledge comes into contradiction with God's Word and nature. We must surrender our own ways for His, and pursue truth with humility and openness to the Holy Spirit's guidance.

In a 2010 article in *America Magazine*, written by James Martin, S.J. (2010) tells a story about John Kavanaugh, a famous ethicist, who on a journey to Calcutta in search of Mother Teresa and a higher purpose. He spent three months working at "the house of the dying," hoping to discover how best to spend the rest of his life. Upon meeting Mother Teresa, he humbly asked her to pray for him.

When she asked him what he wanted her to pray for, he replied, "Clarity. Pray that I have clarity." But to his surprise, Mother Teresa refused his request. "Clarity is the last thing you are clinging to and must let go of," she said, explaining her refusal. Kavanaugh was taken aback and asked why clarity was not something to strive for. Mother Teresa replied, "I have never had clarity; what I have always had is trust. So I will pray that you trust God."

This story highlights the importance of trusting God's plan, even in the face of uncertainty and lack of clarity. We often seek clarity and knowledge to give us a sense of control, but it is ultimately trust in God that brings peace and fulfillment. Clarity is often desired when judgment is seen as our job rather than God's.

We all seem to have a tendency to want to be the judge, don't we? Whether it's judging situations, people, or even ourselves, we fall into the trap of thinking it's our responsibility to make those calls. Here's the thing: just like in any other profession, if I were given a job description and neglected the duties laid out for me, my boss wouldn't applaud my creativity in doing other tasks. Instead, he would reprimand me for neglecting the work I was hired to do and tell me to stay in my lane. If I were a chef and decided to take over the restaurant's marketing instead of cooking, or if I were a teacher and spent my time filing papers instead of educating, my boss would tell me to focus on what I was hired to do… teach. Similarly, Jesus gave us one simple yet profound job: love God and love people. And yet, 2,000 years later, we continue to avoid the very task He gave us, endlessly trying to take on roles that aren't ours. Maybe, just maybe, if we could get this one job right, He would trust us with more. *But until we stop trying to do His job and start focusing on our own, we'll find ourselves distracted and off course.*

It's time to lay down the weight of judgment. Trusting God alleviates the burden we were never meant to bear. It frees us of a weight far too heavy to carry. A return to the garden means we allow God to do the heavy lifting for us once again. Nothing brings Him greater joy than this.

Do you feel weary, heavy-laden, and burdened down? If so, a return to the garden changes everything. Jesus Himself said:

Matthew 11:28
"Come to Me, all of you who are burdened down, and I will give you rest."

You've carried the weight of judge for far too long. It's time to receive the rest that only exists in the Kingdom of God. It is time to return to the garden.

But what does it mean to return to the garden? The garden represents a place of peace, rest, and total trust in God. The garden was where Adam and Eve walked in complete fellowship with God, without shame or fear. It was where they could enjoy the beauty of God's creation without any burden or responsibility. However, the moment they ate from the tree of the knowledge of good and evil, they were no longer able to trust God completely. They had taken on a weight they were never meant to carry, and as a result, they were burdened with shame, fear, and a sense of guilt. They were no longer able to enjoy the beauty of God's creation without the burden of responsibility.

The same is true for us. When we take on the burden of judging what is good and what is evil, we lose our ability to trust in God completely. We become burdened with shame, fear, and guilt. But when we return to the garden, we can once again experience the peace, rest, and complete trust in God that we were created to enjoy. This does not mean all things are good. It means that we trust God to guide our lives and we allow Him to be the judge.

Returning to the garden means laying down our burden of judgment and trusting in God completely. It means recognizing that we are not the judge, but that God has the ultimate authority to judge what is good and what is evil. In fact, in the book of 1 John, it states that:

1 John 1:5
"God is light; in him there is no darkness at all."

God is the very essence of goodness and light, and it is only through Him that we can fully understand what is truly good.

The burden of judgment is not one that we were ever meant to carry, and it is a weight that we cannot bear on our own. As human beings, we are limited in our understanding and wisdom, and we are prone to making mistakes and misjudgments. But when we put our trust in God, we can rest assured that He will guide us and lead us on the right path.

Proverbs 3:5-6
"Trust in the Lord with all your heart and lean not on your own understanding; in all your ways submit to him, and he will make your

paths straight."

When we trust in the Lord and submit to His will, we can be confident that He will guide us on the right path. God, the righteous judge.

It's important to note that the fall of man was not just about Adam and Eve disobeying God's commandment not to eat from the tree of the knowledge of good and evil. It was about the desire for knowledge and power, and the temptation to be “like God.” Isn’t it wild that Satan tempts us with our very identity? Adam and Eve were already made in the image of God, yet Satan comes in, questions God, questions our identity, and tries to offer something that God had already given them! It’s almost as if the enemy’s strategy is to make us forget who we truly are and to convince us that we are missing something. In fact, in Genesis 3, the serpent tempted Eve by saying:

Genesis 3:5
"For God knows that when you eat from it your eyes will be opened, and you will be like God, knowing good and evil."

This desire for knowledge and power is a temptation we all face, and it is a reminder to be careful not to become prideful or self-reliant.

Proverbs 16:18
"Pride goes before destruction, a haughty spirit before a fall."

When we rely on our own understanding and seek to be our own judge, we are setting ourselves up for a fall. The only way to avoid this is to surrender our pride and submit to God's will. It is only through Him that we can find true wisdom, understanding, and guidance. As James reminded us in His letter to the early church:

James 1:5
"If any of you lacks wisdom, you should ask God, who gives generously to all without finding fault, and it will be given to you."

I love taking my son, Kye, to the playground. His favorite thing to do is to climb the jungle gym and slide down the twisty slide. One day, when he was about 4 years old, we saw a group of older kids on the monkey bars. They looked so cool, flipping and hanging upside down. Kye decided he wanted to be like them and try it out for himself.

He climbed up the ladder and grabbed onto the first bar. As soon as he lifted his feet, I saw the rush of excitement on his face. But as he reached for the second bar, I could see he was struggling. He didn't know how to swing his body or hold on tight enough. Panic set in, and he froze. He tried to call for help, but his voice was stuck in his throat.

Eventually, one of the older kids noticed him and came to his rescue. As she helped him down, she said, "You have to be careful up there. It's not as easy as it looks." Kye learned a valuable lesson that day. Just because something looks fun or exciting doesn't mean it's right for him. He had to be responsible and make choices based on his abilities and limitations, not just his desires.

Similarly, when Adam and Eve tasted the fruit from the tree of knowledge, they were not prepared for the responsibility that came with it. They thought they could handle the weight of judging good and evil, but they quickly realized they were in over their heads. They had to face the consequences of their actions and the burden of their newfound knowledge. They learned the hard way that knowledge comes with responsibility and that we must be careful what we reach for. We must be responsible and make choices based on God's guidance, not just our desires.

Again, the fall of man was not just a simple act of disobedience, but a reminder of the burden of judgment that we were never meant to carry. When we take on the responsibility of judging, we are weighed down by something God never intended for us to bear. But by putting our trust in God, surrendering our pride, and seeking truth, we can find rest and guidance in Him. Let me remind you once more of Jesus' words in the gospel of Matthew:

Matthew 11:28-30

"Come to me, all you who are weary and burdened, and I will give you rest. Take my yoke upon you and learn from me, for I am gentle and humble in heart, and you will find rest for your souls. For my yoke is easy and my burden is light."

Section Two: Death

When man and woman leave the Garden, they entered a grave. A place where death is imminent and yet God is still gracious. When separated from the "Tree of Life," survival seems to become our instinct rather than our dependence on God.

Chapter Four: A Holding Pattern

Does it ever feel like no matter what you do, and despite your best attempts, you're just surviving instead of thriving? Does it seem like the abundant life you keep hearing about is really far away? That it can't truly be attained? If so, you are not alone. Many of us have experienced these feelings at some point in our lives.

When Adam and Eve tasted the forbidden fruit, they went into survival mode. Being separated from the garden, the place where the tree of life resided, they were forced to fend for themselves. There's a reason the scriptures remind us that the wage of sin is death. You and I are always being given the choice to choose either life or death. Truthfully, there really is no in between. It's always one or the other, and there really is no grey area. When Adam and Eve stepped away from the garden that contained the tree of life, they entered a grave. They moved from a garden to a grave, from life to death.

The wage of sin is death. We seem all too familiar with this passage of Scripture. We seem to know innately that sin leads us to death. However, I believe that we've misinterpreted this passage of Scripture. We've misread this passage for years, in fact. We know the payment for sin is death, but this passage reveals that sin actually produces death, just as a job produces pay. When we work, we receive a certain wage.

The wage, you see, is just a byproduct of the actions taken. Sin will always receive its wage. Death will always catch up to sin.

In the Old Testament, we see God establish Covenants that are full of laws and regulations geared toward helping to keep us safe from sin, receiving its wage. This was God's way of getting us into position of protection and provision. Contrary to how it might look on the surface, this covenant is not a checklist of "dos and don'ts" implemented by a tyrannical God. Instead, on the contrary, this is a gracious covenant that clings to the promise that God makes throughout scriptureI *"If you will be my people, I will be your God."* This is the thread we see run from the beginning to the end of Scripture.

Exodus 6:7
"I will take you as my own people, and I will be your God. Then you will know that I am the Lord your God, who brought you out from under the yoke of the Egyptians."

Leviticus 26:12
"I will walk among you and be your God, and you will be my people."

Jeremiah 7:23

"but I gave them this command: Obey me, and I will be your God and you will be my people. Walk in obedience to all I command you, that it may go well with you."

Jeremiah 11:4
"I said, 'Obey me and do everything I command you, and you will be my people, and I will be your God.'"

Jeremiah 24:7
"I will give them a heart to know me, that I am the Lord. They will be my people, and I will be their God, for they will return to me with all their heart."

Jeremiah 30:22
"So you will be my people, and I will be your God."

Jeremiah 31:33
"I will be their God, and they will be my people."

Ezekiel 11:20
"They will be my people, and I will be their God."

Ezekiel 14:11
"They will be my people, and I will be their God, declares the Sovereign

Lord."

Ezekiel 36:28

"Then you will live in the land I gave your ancestors; you will be my people, and I will be your God."

Ezekiel 37:23

"... or I will save them from all their sinful backsliding, and I will cleanse them. They will be my people, and I will be their God."

Ezekiel 37:27

"... or I will save them from all their sinful backsliding, and I will cleanse them. They will be my people, and I will be their God."

Hosea 2:23

"I will plant her for myself in the land; I will show my love to the one I called 'Not my loved one. I will say to those called 'Not my people,' 'You are my people'; and they will say, 'You are my God.'"

Zechariah 8:8

"I will bring them back to live in Jerusalem; they will be my people, and I will be faithful and righteous to them as their God."

Zechariah 13:9

"They will call on my name and I will answer them; I will say, 'They are my people,' and they will say, 'The Lord is our God.'"

2 Corinthians 6:16
"I will live with them and walk among them, and I will be their God, and they will be my people."

Hebrews 8:10
"This is the covenant I will establish with the people of Israel after that time, declares the Lord I will put my laws in their minds and write them on their hearts. I will be their God, and they will be my people."

Revelation 21:1-3
"Then I saw 'a new heaven and a new earth,' for the first heaven and the first earth had passed away, and there was no longer any sea. I saw the Holy City, the new Jerusalem, coming down out of heaven from God, prepared as a bride beautifully dressed for her husband. And I heard a loud voice from the throne saying, 'Look! God's dwelling place is now among the people, and he will dwell with them. They will be his people, and God himself will be with them and be their God.

In the heart of God lies an unquenchable desire: to be your God and for you to be His people. He made a covenant with humanity to ensure that we may live without the crushing weight of sin. You see, because we've bought into a false narrative concerning God, we sometimes look to the rules and regulations of the Old Testament and think that God is just some tyrant who never wants us to have any fun. That simply isn't the case. In fact, even the covenant within the Old Testament reminds us of the good. This old covenant is a means of grace that held us in a holding pattern, protecting us from the just punishment of sin. And then came the day that God fulfilled His promise and sent His Son, Jesus Christ, to give sin its final wage.

The covenant placed a hedge around God's people in order to protect our sinful nature from the inevitable death that is always produced by sin. Remember, there is no escaping the wage of sin on our own. The reason we struggle with how God is portrayed in the Old Testament is that we misunderstand the covenant.

To understand some of the difficult passages in the Old Testament, we must view them in their proper context. Many times, we see accounts of mass genocide or a portrayal of God as cruel and unloving. However, we must remember that sin always leads to death. In the Old Testament, the covenant was a hedge of protection that prevented death from catching up to sin.

Throughout the Old Testament, we see God pleading with his people to remain under the covenant. In Exodus 19:5-6, God tells the Israelites, "Now if you obey me fully and keep my covenant, then out of all nations you will be my treasured possession. Although the whole earth is mine, you will be for me a kingdom of priests and a holy nation." This covenant was established by God to protect His people from the consequences of their sins.

When we see God depicted as ungracious and unloving in the Old Testament, we miss the bigger picture. God was constantly urging His people to remain under the covenant, because He knew that without it, death would consume them. God's plea for His people to remain under the covenant was an act of grace and love, because all they had to do was obey and trust in Him to be protected from the consequences of their sins.

In Deuteronomy 30:19-20, God says, "This day I call the heavens and the earth as witnesses against you that I have set before you life and death, blessings and curses. Now choose life, so that you and your children may live and that you may love the Lord your God, listen to his voice, and hold fast to him." God's desire was for His people to choose life by remaining under the covenant and trusting in Him.

It is important to remember that the covenant was not meant to be a burden or a restriction, but rather a means of protection from the consequences of sin. The covenant was established by God as a means of protection for His people. The covenant was not meant to be a burden or a restriction, but rather an act of grace and love from God to His people.

Let's take a moment to think about a fish in a bowl. If the fish stays in the water, it can survive and live a full life. However, the moment the fish tries to live outside of the water, he perishes. Interestingly, we don't hear the fish complain to its owners, saying, "You're so cruel for keeping me in this water! I want to be free! Let me breathe the toxic air!" Instead, the fish understands that staying in the bowl, in its natural habitat, is where it can thrive.

In the same way, some of us view the old covenant as restrictive instead of life-giving. But we need to remember that, just as the bowl kept the fish from death, the old covenant kept us safe from the dangers of sin. Sin always has consequences, and the old covenant was a means of grace that protected us from the harm that sin can bring.

There are three key figures during this "holding pattern" who help God's people understand His desires, faithfulness, power, and passions. These three people are the prophets, priests, and kings. The revelations spoken by the prophets allowed God's people to understand His desires for them. The priest's role allowed them to understand His faithfulness, and the king's authority gave them a sense of His power and passions. They had to walk truly by faith, not by sight. People didn't have this "personal" relationship with God. Their relationship was lived out through these prophets, priests, and kings. But God's covenant is a reminder of His goodness, even when we do not see or feel His presence.

Hebrews 8:7-9 states that the covenant established by God had no fault. The covenant was not the issue. The issue was who it was made with. The fault was brought by man, not by God. Therefore, our shortcomings are not a defining factor in God's character, and God did not fail. Once again, we failed. A covenant is not something to be broken or used for selfish gain. Instead, God pursued us to keep the covenant intact.

So, if we feel that Christianity is burdensome, we may be missing the invitation of the New Covenant. There are three burdens that may identify our connection to the old covenant:

1. We cannot hear God.
2. We cannot talk to God.
3. We cannot walk with God.

The prophets heard from God, the priests talked to God, and the kings walked with God. However, only a handful of people could walk with God before the new covenant. Therefore, the world felt the burden of not being able to walk with God.

In the midst of our struggle to communicate with God, it's important to remember that the breakdown in communication is not God's fault nor that of the prophets. Rather, it's a result of our own shortcomings. However, there is hope for those of us living under the old covenant. Paul recognized that the new covenant made with Jesus provides a way for us to experience true freedom in Christ. The Greek word for Christ, "*Christos,*" signifies that Jesus suffered and rose again from the dead, overcoming the burdens that once controlled our lives. Jesus is our Prophet, Priest, and King, and through Him, we can now approach God with confidence. Scripture tells us that Jesus did not abandon us but instead provided a new way, a new covenant. In John 14:6, Jesus says, "I am the way, the truth, and the life. No one comes to the Father except through me." Without the way, there is no path forward; without the truth, there is no clear direction, and without Life, there is no future. Jesus is the answer!

That is good news! The good news is that Jesus removed the failure to keep the covenant and that God is always working, even in our waiting. We must stop trying to survive and learn that God is a God who provides. We know that the old covenant was only temporary. It was a holding pattern until Jesus could pay sin its wage. His sacrifice on the cross gave us access to a new covenant, one that allows us to thrive even more fully in our relationship with God. So let us not view the old covenant as restrictive but as a gracious protection that ultimately led us to a deeper, more meaningful connection with our Heavenly Father. All because His initial desire is His final intent.

It's important to understand that this doesn't mean you won't face challenges, difficulties, or even periods of waiting. In fact, waiting is often a necessary part of the process, and it's during these times that we may feel like we're in a holding pattern. We may wonder whether we'll ever break free and experience the abundant life we were created for.

The truth is, waiting can be frustrating and uncomfortable. But it's also a time when God is working behind the scenes, preparing us for what's to come. Just as the covenant in the Old Testament was a holding pattern that created protection, the waiting periods in our lives are also holding patterns that prepare us for what's next.

In the Bible, we see many examples of people who experienced waiting periods. Joseph spent years in prison before becoming second-in-command in Egypt. Moses spent 40 years in the wilderness before leading the Israelites out of Egypt. David, too, spent many years on the run before becoming king. These individuals experienced periods of waiting, but they also trusted in God's plan for their lives.

We may not always understand why we're waiting, but we can trust that God has a purpose for it. It's during these times that we can learn to rely on God and grow in our faith. We can seek His guidance and direction, and allow Him to work in our lives in ways that we may not have experienced otherwise.

When we feel like we're in a holding pattern, it's important to remember that God is always at work. He hasn't forgotten about us or our desires. He's preparing us for what's next, and He will bring us into the fullness of the abundant life that He has promised. We may be observing the Garden at a distance, but God is making a way. We see the Psalmist, one who experienced the covenants of old, write in Psalm 23:3 “He restores my soul; He leads me in the paths of righteousness For His name’s sake.” God is recalibrating our paths and restoring all things back to their initial design and intent.

In the New Testament, we see the ultimate example of waiting and preparation in the earthly life of Jesus. He spent 30 years in obscurity before beginning His public ministry. During this time, He was preparing for His ultimate mission - to offer Himself as a sacrifice for the sins of the world. To remove the failures of man so that the new covenant would not be reliant on our ability to uphold the covenant. Jesus’ example teaches us that waiting is not a wasted time. It's a time of preparation, growth, and trust in God's plan for our lives. And just as Jesus' waiting period led to the ultimate victory over sin and death, our waiting periods can lead to victory and fulfillment in our own lives.

So if you're feeling like you're in a holding pattern, don't lose hope. Trust in God's plan, seek His guidance, and allow Him to work in your life during this time of preparation. And remember, God's desire for you is not just to survive, but to thrive and experience the fullness of the abundant life that He has promised. Again, let us embrace the new covenant made possible through Jesus and approach God with the assurance of His grace and mercy. The old is gone, the new has come!

Chapter Five: Making Poor Trades

As humans, we often make poor judgments when it comes to cutting deals and making bargains. We tend to sell ourselves short, even when we think we are getting the deal of a lifetime. This is especially true when it comes to the journey of faith, as we have bought into a false narrative and have believed the lies of Satan. As a result, we have traded priceless treasures for something of far less value.

One of the earliest examples of this can be seen in the story of Adam and Eve in the Garden of Eden. They traded life for death by eating the forbidden fruit, believing the lie that they would be like God. Similarly, the story of Judas comes to mind, as he traded his closeness to Jesus for 30 pieces of silver.

It's amazing how the name Judas has become synonymous with betrayal and treachery. Even those who have never read the Bible or know nothing about Jesus wouldn't name their child Judas. It's a universally agreed-upon fact that Judas is "the worst." In fact, the name Judas is so rare that it's on the brink of extinction. According to the Social Security Administration, no babies were named Judas in the United States in 2020. And in 2019, only five babies were given this name. 2020 was a hard enough year! Thank God no one had a Judas! Poor Judas, his legacy will always be tied to the ultimate act of betrayal. But let's be honest, if anyone ever tells you that they are naming their child Judas, you might judge their decision-making skills.

Judas, one of the twelve apostles, was also entrusted by Jesus with the mission of spreading the gospel, and he performed miracles just like the others. However, his story took a tragic turn, and he is often remembered for betraying Jesus for 30 pieces of silver. It's easy to look down on Judas for his actions, but the truth is that we are not so different from him. We, too, make mistakes and fall short in our faith. We may not betray Jesus for money, but we may prioritize other things over him. If we are being honest, we have traded Jesus for far less than 30 pieces of silver.

We have already established that we are bad judges. We misjudge what we need and what God has for us, which leads us to sell ourselves short. We need to be aware that Satan loves nothing more than to convince us that we are getting the deal of a lifetime when it comes to sin. Although it may feel good in the moment, it ultimately leaves us with nothing except death.

In contrast, God is offering us a way to trade our kingdoms for His. He is offering us a better deal than anything we could imagine, but we often fail to recognize this. We are too busy holding on to our own kingdoms that we forget Jesus is giving us the keys to His Kingdom.

When my wife, Cassidy, was younger, she faced a decision that would shape the course of her life. Her mother gave her two options: a weekly allowance to spend on anything she wanted, or the ability to come to her mother whenever she had a need, and let her mother decide whether or not to purchase what Cassidy really wanted.

Cassidy, like any young person, thought that the weekly allowance was the deal of a lifetime. She could make her own decisions and have the freedom to do what she wanted with the money. She took the weekly allowance and started making decisions for herself. But what she didn't realize was that the money would never be enough to fulfill all her desires.

As the weeks went by, she spent the money on movies with friends and milkshakes at Johnny Rockets. But soon, the money ran out, and she was left with nothing. She realized too late that it would have been wiser to go to her mother whenever she needed anything or whenever she wanted something. Her mother had the wisdom to know what was best for her and the resources to provide for her needs.

This story is a personal analogy about how we as humans often trade the presence of God for the things of God. We think that we can handle our lives on our own, making our own decisions without seeking God's guidance. But just like Cassidy's weekly allowance, the things of God, apart from the presence of God, will never fulfill all our desires. We must instead rely on God's presence and trust in His wisdom and provision for our lives.

When we seek God's presence and trust in His guidance, He provides us with all that we need. But when we try to take the things of God without being in His presence, we will always come up wanting. Let us remember to depend on God and not trade the things of God for His presence.

God is offering us the deal of a lifetime, but we need to be willing to trade our kingdoms for His. It is like going to a pawn shop with a priceless piece of jewelry. The person behind the counter is always willing to cut a deal, but it is never a good deal for the person trading the priceless jewelry. In the same way, sin may feel good in the moment, but it ultimately leaves us with nothing. We need to recognize that God's way is the only way that leads to true life and fulfillment.

In the book of Matthew, Jesus tells a parable about a man who found a treasure hidden in a field. He sold everything he had to buy the field, because he recognized the value of the treasure. We must have the same perspective on the Kingdom of God. It is worth trading everything we have to obtain it, because it is the only thing that truly matters. We need to be aware of the poor trades we make in our lives, and recognize that God is offering us something far better. We must become willing to trade our kingdoms for His and recognize that His way is the only way to true life and fulfillment. May we have the courage and wisdom to make the right trades and follow Jesus on the journey of faith.

The Bible tells us that "the wages of sin is death, but the gift of God is eternal life in[a] Christ Jesus our Lord." (Romans 6:23). Jesus Christ is the ultimate and most valuable treasure that we can ever receive. Yet, we so often trade His love, grace, and salvation for temporary pleasures, sin, and the false promises of the world. We must understand that the world and everything in it is temporary and will one day pass away, but God and His Kingdom are eternal. We cannot afford to make poor trades with our souls and exchange the eternal for the temporary. Instead, we must seek to gain the Kingdom of God and all its righteousness, which will never pass away.

One of the greatest examples of someone who made a wise trade in the Bible is the apostle Paul. Before he became a Christian, Paul was a devout Jew and a Pharisee who zealously persecuted the early Christian church. But when he encountered Jesus Christ on the road to Damascus, Paul had a change of heart and surrendered his life to Christ. Paul gave up his former way of life, his status as a highly respected Pharisee, and his own personal gain for the sake of knowing Christ and sharing the gospel with others.

In his letter to the Philippians, Paul writes, "But whatever gain I had, I counted as loss for the sake of Christ. Indeed, I count everything as loss because of the surpassing worth of knowing Christ Jesus my Lord. For his sake I have suffered the loss of all things and count them as rubbish, in order that I may gain Christ" (Philippians 3:7-8).

Paul understood that all his former accomplishments, possessions, and status were of little value compared to the priceless treasure of knowing and serving Jesus Christ. He willingly gave up everything to follow

Christ and fulfill His purpose for his life.

We must also be willing to make wise trades in our own lives to give up anything that hinders us from following Christ wholeheartedly. We may need to let go of relationships, habits, desires, and even possessions that are keeping us from living for Christ. We must be willing to count everything as loss for the sake of gaining Christ and His Kingdom.

We must be careful not to make poor trades in our lives, especially when it comes to our relationship with God. We must seek to gain the Kingdom of God and all its righteousness, which is eternal, and not trade it for temporary pleasures or the false promises of the world. We must be willing to give up anything that hinders us from following Christ wholeheartedly and to count everything as loss for the sake of gaining Christ. May we be wise traders and seek to honor and please God in all that we do.

Although we sometimes like to give Judas a very bad rap for betraying Jesus, the reality is that in our walk of faith as Christians, so many times we do the exact same thing. Often without ever even realizing it. We trade Jesus for the things of this world. And when we do, we have nothing to show for it. We make very poor trades. It's time to remember that God knows better. He always has, and He always will. Again, trust is not about knowing what God knows, but about knowing that God knows. If you're tired of selling yourself short and living a life with very little to show for it, it's time to return to the garden. Remember, God isn't trying to take away from you. God is trying to give to you. And even if what you have right now seems good, I promise you, my friend, there's something far, far better. God's way is always better.

As a watch enthusiast on a budget, I am always on the lookout for the perfect deal. One day, a friend suggested I check out estate sales for vintage watches. So, when I heard about an estate sale featuring a watch enthusiast who had passed away, I knew I had to check it out. Unfortunately, I arrived an hour late, and all the watches were gone. I was crestfallen as I saw the empty watch boxes strewn on the ground, each representing a missed opportunity. But as I glanced around, something else caught my eye: a set of Callaway golf clubs being sold for just $100.

I bought the clubs with the intention of reselling them for a profit or trading them for something else. However, a few months later, I decided to use the clubs for a golf outing. As I moved my golf balls and other gear into the bag, I unzipped a small, velvet-lined pouch and pulled out a mint-condition Tudor Blackbay 58 watch. This was a dream watch worth over $4,000.

I immediately contacted the estate sale company to let them know I had found an extra watch in the bag and wanted to pay them for it. However, to my surprise, they replied with a simple message: "All sales are final." Apparently, everything in the bag, including the extra watch, was included in the sale.

As I reflected on this experience, I realized it was a lot like our faith. We can embrace the idea of eternal life through Jesus' sacrifice, but we often fail to realize that He has called us to experience more of His kingdom here on earth. We have access to the abundance of the Garden, but when we live in complacency and settle for less, we miss out on the fullness of life that Jesus offers.

When we come to God with excuses about why we're not worthy or why we can't pursue the "more" that He promises, He simply responds: "All sales are final." Jesus paid the ultimate price on the cross, and we have been bought with a price. We have the choice to either accept the fullness of what Jesus purchased for us or continue to live as slaves to our sin. The choice is ours, but all sales are final.

Chapter Six: Division or Diversity

I have a confession to make. You've reached what I think is my favorite chapter in this whole book. Personally, I love it because it's so relatable. I think you'll soon see why.

In Genesis 3:12-13, when God asked Eve what she had done, her first response was to blame someone else. Have you been there? The truth is, as humans, we have a very selfish nature. And when standing before a rightful, righteous judge ourselves, our go-to response is to immediately cast blame on someone else. We see this even in the church.

Satan uses our selfish nature to condemn others before we stand before the rightful Judge ourselves. After eating from the forbidden fruit, we blamed others instead of taking responsibility. It's all too common, really, and we still see it today. When we are in survival mode, we try to pass the blame to avoid repercussions for our actions, all while holding someone else accountable for their shortcomings. We do this to take the focus off ourselves. Passing the blame is an active decision to divide rather than unite.

The root of division and diversity is the same: differences. It's not the differences themselves that are problematic, but rather how we respond to them. We have a choice to make: we can either celebrate our differences as evidence of God's unique and intentional design, or we can create divisions based on similarities. It is our selfish nature that leads us to divide rather than embrace diversity. Differences exist, but it's up to us what we do with them. Our differences can bring division and shame, or diversity and unity. In the Garden, the unity experienced was the result of leveraging differences for the Kingdom rather than dividing the Kingdom into territories that no longer resemble God's initial creation or design.

The Bible tells us that even life in the Kingdom is filled with great diversity. We're all so very different, but everyone has something to offer. It's time to return to the place of unity by realizing that it was never our role to be the judge in the first place.

In the early church, there was great diversity. With so many coming into the faith, there were differences everywhere. In fact, even then, differences seemed to abound. No two believers were the same. But they were all together in one accord and had all things in common. This does not mean that everyone was identical. It simply means that, despite all the differences, they focused on what they had in common. Jesus. Their willingness to have all things in common was a deep-rooted desire to find common ground. As they gazed upon the Kingdom of God with great clarity, the trivialities of this world faded away. In that moment, they recognized that their shared faith in Jesus was their true commonality, the only thing that truly mattered.

Today, unfortunately, even after all these centuries, we're still so concerned with focusing on differences rather than on what keeps us together. Because of the false narrative, we see differences and then create division. Friends, it's time to return to the place of unity.

In 1 Corinthians 12:12-14, Paul compares the church to a body. He says, *"For just as the body is one and has many members, and all the members of the body, though many, are one body, so it is with Christ. For in one Spirit we were all baptized into one body--Jews or Greeks, slaves or free--and all were made to drink of one Spirit. For the body does not consist of one member but of many."* Each of us is a part of the body of Christ, and our differences are not meant to divide us, but to work together for the common goal of serving and glorifying God. Each part is different, but each part is necessary for the body to function properly. Just like a body, the church cannot function without all its parts working together.

We need to recognize that our differences are what make us unique and valuable to the Kingdom of God. We all have something to offer, and we need to embrace our differences and work together to achieve a common goal. A garden is most beautiful when it is diverse, and the same goes for the Kingdom of God. When we allow ourselves to be divided, we move away from God's original intent. Instead, we should embrace our differences as important attributes that contribute to the beauty of the Kingdom.

When we allow our selfish nature to take control and start judging others, this not only hinders our ability to serve and glorify God, but it also damages our witness to the world. Jesus himself prayed for unity among believers in John 17:20-23, saying, "I do not ask for these only, but also for those who will believe in me through their word, that they may all be one, just as you, Father, are in me, and I in you, that they also may be in us, so that the world may believe that you have sent me. The glory that you have given me I have given to them, that they may be one even as we are one, I in them and you in me, that they may become perfectly one, so that the world may know that you sent me and loved them even as you loved me."

When we are unified as the body of Christ, we are a powerful witness to the world of Christ's love. This is why it is so important to resist the temptation to judge others and instead focus on what we have in common. As the Apostle Paul writes in Ephesians 4:3, "Make every effort to keep the unity of the Spirit through the bond of peace."

So, how do we resist the temptation to judge others and instead focus on unity?

First and foremost, we need to have a humble attitude. In Philippians 2:3-4, Paul writes, "Do nothing from selfish ambition or conceit, but in humility count others more significant than yourselves. Let each of you look not only to his own interests, but also to the interests of others." When we approach others with humility and a willingness to serve, we are less likely to judge them.

Secondly, we need to remember that we are all sinners in need of grace. Romans 3:23 says, "For all have sinned and fall short of the glory of God." We aren't perfect, and we all need the grace of God in our lives. When we remember this, we are more likely to extend grace to others.

Finally, we need to focus on what we have in common. As followers of Christ, we all have a common bond in our faith. We are all united by our belief in Jesus Christ as our Lord and Savior. When we focus on this common bond, we are less likely to be divided by our differences.

As a musician, I reminisce about my time in a band, and I can't help but draw a parallel between our band's dynamics and the concept of unity among believers in Christ. If you picture a band on stage, you'll see so many people, each with their unique talents and instruments. From the guitarist to the bass player, there's a beautiful diversity that makes each member essential to the whole.

When each musician has their instrument, they have complete freedom to play whatever they desire. They have free will. But something magical happens when every member, regardless of their individual differences, chooses to play the same note. Suddenly, amid the chaos, a harmonious sound begins to emerge. This is the true essence of unity.

For instance, the piano player could easily explore all 88 keys, but instead chooses to play in one accord with their bandmates. The result is beautiful music that's pleasing to the ears. This is precisely what unity looks like, and it's a choice that each member has to make.

When we recognize the power of diversity and choose to come together, something beautiful happens. This is what God intended from the beginning, for us to live in harmony and work together for a common goal. Instead of constantly judging and being judged, it's time to let go of those burdens and come back to the place of unity.

In summary, just like a band on stage, every believer in Christ has a unique set of talents and abilities, but the decision to come together and work as a team is what leads to beautiful things. It's a choice that we must make daily, to let go of our differences and focus on the greater good, and this is the true essence of unity.

Again, let me remind you of the book of Acts. It says that the early church had "all things in common" (Acts 2:44-45). This statement is not just a surface-level observation. It is a profound reflection of the unity that existed among the early believers.

They did not suddenly start enjoying the same food or having the same preferences. Instead, they experienced the Kingdom of God at such a level that the things of this world faded in comparison, and they chose to focus on the one thing that truly mattered: the Kingdom of God. They chose to unite around the one thing they had in common; which was their faith in Christ. They recognized that in Christ, there is neither Jew nor Gentile, slave nor free, male nor female, for all are one in Christ Jesus (Galatians 3:28). They understood that unity in Christ was essential to their witness and testimony to the world.

The early church demonstrated that unity is a choice that believers in Christ must make. It requires putting aside personal preferences and differences and choosing to focus on what we have in common: our faith in Christ and our commitment to His Kingdom. This choice is not always easy, and division is always an option. But we are called to strive for unity, just as Christ prayed for His followers to be one, just as He and the Father are one (John 17:21).

May we, as followers of Christ, choose to prioritize unity in our relationships with one another, as we seek to reflect the unity and love of the Triune God. The temptation to judge others is common and we all face it. However, as Christians, we are called to resist this temptation and instead focus on unity. When we are unified as the body of Christ, we are a powerful witness to the world of Christ's love. May we all strive to resist the temptation to judge others and instead focus on what we have in common as followers of Christ.

So what is the secret to unity? How do we stay unified when differences arise? Continue to gather. If we willingly gather, God will miraculously unite us. A willingness to gather is not the act of ignoring our differences; it is the practice of uniting despite our differences. Differences don't have to lead to division; division is choosing to let our differences define our way of life. Again, differences will lead to division or diversity, and it's our choice. If we choose unity, we will experience diversity, and like every miracle, it must be received and applied.

Have I convinced you that unity is the answer yet? If not, let me offer two reasons why we should long for unity in our faith.

The first is that unity attracts God's blessings. In Psalm 133:1-2, we read, "How good and pleasant it is when God's people live together in unity! It is like precious oil poured on the head, running down on the beard, running down on Aaron's beard, down on the collar of his robe."

Oil is symbolic of the Holy Spirit. On the day of Pentecost, when the believers were in one mind and accord, the Holy Spirit came down. If we want God to empower and bless us, there has to be unity in the church. God cannot bless nor favor division; He is a God of unity. There is unity in the Godhead, and He expects unity among His people. Again, in John 17:20-23, Jesus prays His last prayer and states, "My prayer is not for them alone. I pray also for those who will believe in me through their message, that all of them may be one, Father, just as you are in me and I am in you. May they also be in us so that the world may believe that you have sent me. I have given them the glory that you gave me, that they may be one as we are one. I in them and you in me, so that they may be brought to complete unity. Then the world will know that you sent me and have loved them even as you have loved me."

Secondly, unity leads to multiplication, as we read in Ecclesiastes 4:9, "Two are better than one because they have a good reward for their labor." More can be accomplished when we work together than when we work separately. What I can do is defeating, but what we can do is liberating. When Jesus sent out the disciples, He sent them out two by two because there is strength in numbers. Two is better than one, three is better than two, and so on. Isolation is the same as division, and choosing to be separate is the same as choosing to push others out.

A church that is divided will eventually implode from within and destroy itself. If a church is divided, it will not accomplish what it's supposed to accomplish. A house divided cannot stand or last. Jesus knew this when He said, "Every kingdom divided against itself will be ruined, and every city or household divided against itself will not stand" (Matthew 12:25). One of the biggest warnings I can offer is to avoid gossip, because gossip tears down kingdoms.

Several centuries ago, ancient China faced a constant threat from its northern invaders. To secure their borders, they built the Great Wall of China, an immense fortification. The wall was too high for the enemy to scale, too thick to tear down, and too long to go around. They also posted soldiers at different places to patrol the wall, giving them a superior advantage over their enemies. But, in the first 100 years of the Great Wall's existence, the nation was invaded three times. How did the enemy breach such a seemingly impenetrable barrier? Through division.

An enemy bribed the gatekeepers, causing them to turn a blind eye as the enemy entered undetected. The enemy knew that they could not defeat the unified forces guarding the wall, so they sought to divide them and create an opening. And it worked.

As believers, we must heed this warning. Our enemy, the devil, seeks to destroy the Church and the things of God. And he knows that he cannot defeat a united Church. So, he seeks to divide us and create an opening. He uses our differences in opinions, beliefs, and practices to pit us against each other. But, we must remember that we are one Body in Christ. We may have different roles, but we are all united in our faith. We must strive for unity, not uniformity. We must love one another and work together, despite our differences. Because if we allow division to take hold, we open ourselves up to attack.

Let us be unified in our mission. Let us resist the enemy's attempts to divide us and stand firm in our faith. Only then can we be truly effective in advancing the Kingdom of God. The source of both diversity and division is one and the same – our differences. However, what we choose to do with those differences ultimately determines whether we foster unity or sow discord.

Chapter 7: Personal Faith vs Private Faith

Not long ago, after delivering a sermon at our church, I found myself in a conversation with someone in the lobby. They asked, "Why did Satan choose to tempt Eve instead of Adam?" It's a thought-provoking that honestly led to an intriguing discussion. Although there isn't a definitive answer within the scriptures, I couldn't help but ponder the possibilities.

Genesis 3:1 tells us, *"Now the serpent was more crafty than any of the wild animals the LORD God had made. He said to the woman, 'Did God really say, 'You must not eat from any tree in the garden?'"*

While the scriptures don't provide a clear answer, I have developed some theories that might shed light on this question. It's essential to recognize that theories are not the same as theology. The difference is significant; theories offer possible explanations, while theology is based on authoritative religious teaching.

One theory I propose is that Satan tempted Eve rather than Adam because we never see God instructing Eve directly not to eat the forbidden fruit. While it's clear that Eve knew it was wrong, did she understand it was wrong because God told her, or because Adam relayed the message? Look at Genesis Chapter 2:

Genesis 2:15-17

"The Lord God took the man and put him in the Garden of Eden to work it and take care of it. And the Lord God commanded the man, "You are free to eat from any tree in the garden; but you must not eat from the tree of the knowledge of good and evil, for when you eat from it you will certainly die."

So God clearly told Adam but was Eve present? Look at the next verse, verse 18:

Genesis 2:18

"The Lord God said, "It is not good for the man to be alone. I will make a helper suitable for him.""

Again, this is just a theory, and there is plenty of room for speculation. However, it's interesting to consider that Satan often targets those who believe based on the words of others rather than personal revelation from God. In other words, Satan enjoys exploiting "loopholes" in our faith.

The discoveries we make on our faith journey far outweigh what others tell us. That which is discovered is far greater than that which is merely declared. This is why I felt compelled to include this chapter in the book to emphasize that faith is personal. It's not enough to hear about Jesus; you need to know Jesus for yourself. Knowing about the things of God is one thing, but experiencing them firsthand is an entirely different matter.

We can see this in the story of Philip and the Ethiopian eunuch in Acts 8:26-40. Philip encountered the eunuch, who was reading the Book of Isaiah but struggling to understand its meaning. Philip took the time to explain the scripture to him, and through this interaction, the eunuch came to believe in Jesus and was baptized. This story demonstrates the power of personal revelation and the importance of seeking understanding for ourselves.

In the same vein, consider the story of the woman at the well. Her life was transformed after a single encounter with Jesus. She told others about this remarkable man who changed her life completely. However, it wasn't until they experienced Jesus for themselves that their lives were truly changed. This story demonstrates how faith truly works.

Satan uses apparent "loopholes" to create doubt in our minds. When we base our faith on what others say, Satan will try to make us question what God says by casting doubt on their words. In fact, one of Satan's most potent weapons is questioning what God has already spoken. When God's voice is clear, the enemy wants us to doubt it.

We must recognize God's voice as our ultimate and only authority; otherwise, it becomes easy to dismiss when questioned. I believe that part of the reason Satan questioned Eve apart from Adam was that he knew God had already instructed Adam not to eat the fruit. However, Eve had only heard this command from Adam, not directly from God. This created the loophole: "Did God really say, 'You must not eat from any tree in the garden?'" This is why it's crucial for us to know God and His word personally.

Reflect on the example of Jesus' baptism by John. When Jesus was baptized in the Jordan River, God said, "This is my Son, whom I love; with him, I am well pleased."

Just a few verses later, while Jesus was in the desert, Satan began raising questions about what God had initially spoken. "If you are the

Son of God..." This serves as a powerful reminder not to let Satan make us question in the desert what God spoke at the river. We must stand firm in our faith, trusting in God's word and our personal relationship with Him.

Another theory I have is that Satan knew he needed to divide Adam and Eve to destroy them. To achieve this, he targeted Eve. We often trade our "personal faith" for "private faith," but these two concepts are vastly different. Personal faith can be questioned and held accountable, while private faith remains hidden from others, providing no opportunity for discussion or questioning. A person with personal faith takes responsibility for their beliefs, while someone with private faith might argue, "No one can hold me responsible... it's private!"

Personal faith can be public, shared, and enriched through fellowship with others, while private faith cannot. As our faith becomes more private, we risk building our lives on Godly principles instead of on God Himself. Eve knew the Godly answer but was manipulated by the cunning serpent. She began to settle for a view of the garden instead of life within the Garden. This is a pattern we often fall into today. Remember, Satan is crafty and cunning! Godly things are not a substitute for God Himself.

Keeping God in sight but out of reach leads us to observe our faith instead of receiving the blessings that come by faith. This is what happens when we settle for a view of the Garden without personally experiencing the Garden for ourselves. It becomes easy to be deceived by the enemy's schemes. My friend, if you genuinely want to thrive in the Garden and experience all the abundant life God has to offer, you must know the Gardener personally and not merely rely on someone else's word.

You have not only been given the opportunity to return to the Garden, but you have also been invited to know the Gardener personally! It's time to stop taking everyone else's word for it. Chances are, for far too long, you've allowed your faith to be determined by what others say about God. I assure you, once you get to know Him for yourself, you will be amazed by what He has to offer you. When you know God personally and stop relying on others' words, you will find that life in the Garden is far better than any life you could create for yourself, and you will realize that the Gardener has had an incredible plan for your life all along.

Now let's revisit the other possible explanation I mentioned earlier. Satan knew he had to divide Adam and Eve to destroy them, which is why he targeted Eve. We often trade our "personal faith" for a "private faith," but these two concepts are very different. Personal faith allows for questioning and accountability, while private faith keeps beliefs hidden from others. Satan loves nothing more than to divide us, as he is a master manipulator and deceiver, always sowing seeds of division.

This is why it's essential to have accountability in our lives. Faith in God is personal, but it should never be private. We need each other for support, encouragement, and accountability. As we journey together in our faith, we can grow closer to the Gardener and experience the fullness of life in the Garden. By knowing God personally and embracing a personal, shared faith, we can overcome the enemy's attempts to divide and conquer.

Whether Satan targeted Eve because of a loophole in the chain of command or to create division between her and Adam, the important lesson we can draw from this story is the necessity of personal faith. Our faith must be based on our own relationship with God and our experiences with Him. As we cultivate our personal faith and share it with others, we build a strong foundation that withstands the enemy's attacks.

Throughout history, many people have found strength and encouragement by sharing their faith with others. The early church, as described in the Book of Acts, was characterized by fellowship, breaking bread together, and praying for one another. This sense of community and shared faith enabled believers to face persecution and trials with courage and resilience. Likewise, in our modern-day context, we can experience the same strength and unity through personal faith and shared experiences with our fellow believers.

In our pursuit of personal faith, it's important to engage in spiritual practices that foster a deeper connection with God. Prayer, Bible study, worship, and service are all essential components of a thriving spiritual life. As we engage in these practices, we not only deepen our personal faith but also strengthen our connections with other believers, fostering a sense of community and accountability.

Additionally, we must be intentional about sharing our faith with others. In a world where many people experience loneliness and isolation, building relationships with fellow believers can be a lifeline. By sharing our faith journey and offering encouragement, support, and accountability, we help others grow in their faith and experience the fullness of life in the Garden.

As we cultivate personal faith and share it with others, we can overcome the enemy's attempts to divide and conquer. We can experience the fullness of life in the Garden and the joy of knowing the Gardener personally. We must not settle for merely observing our faith or relying on the words and experiences of others. Instead, let us pursue a deep, personal relationship with God and embrace the beauty of shared faith and community.

In the end, our goal is not only to return to the Garden but also to know the Gardener intimately. This personal, experiential knowledge of God is the foundation of a thriving, resilient faith that can withstand the enemy's attacks and deceptions. By nurturing our personal faith, we can enter the Garden and experience its abundant life, not merely as observers but as active participants in God's Kingdom.

May this chapter serve as an invitation and encouragement to pursue personal faith and share it with others. Don't let your faith be determined by what others say about God; instead, seek to know Him personally and experience His presence in your life. As you do, you will find that life in the Garden is more abundant, fulfilling, and joyful than anything the world can offer. Embrace the invitation to know the Gardener, and let your personal faith lead you into the fullness of life in the Kingdom of God.

Again the story of Satan tempting Eve rather than Adam serves as a powerful reminder of the importance of personal faith. Regardless of the reason for Satan's choice, we must recognize the critical role of personal faith in our lives. By seeking God for ourselves and not relying solely on the words of others, we can experience a more profound and transformative faith that withstands the enemy's attacks. By cultivating a personal faith, we can fully embrace the beauty of life in the Garden and the joy of knowing the Gardener intimately. So, let us not settle for a mere view of the Garden but rather pursue a life within it, hand-in-hand with the Gardener Himself.

Section Three: Redeemed

When Jesus stepped out of the grave, He opened the way back to the Garden. Redemption is not merely forgiveness from sin, but restoration to God's original intent. Through Christ, what was broken by the fall is being made new again.

Chapter 8: The Great Reversal

I love movies. Have you ever found yourself immersed in a book or captivated by a movie, all the while knowing the conclusion before the story even unfolds? Either someone spoiled the ending, the storyline was obvious, or the story started by showing you the ending. This storytelling technique is called "*in medias res.*" Its purpose is to create suspense or deepen the narrative's emotional impact by allowing the audience to understand the how and why of the events that lead up to the opening scenes. This technique can make the unfolding of the story more engaging and compelling, as the audience knows where the story is heading but not how it will get there. We see this in films like *Memento, Eternal Sunshine of the Spotless Mind, The Prestige,* and many more.

Knowing the end of the story can provide a unique perspective, allowing us to see the threads of redemption and hope that run through even the darkest moments. As Christians, we find ourselves in a similar situation with the story of our own redemption. We know the end of the story, and this knowledge enables us to live with hope and purpose, even in the face of adversity. We do not just know the ending because of our faith story, but also because the beginning matches the ending. God's initial intent is His final decision.

So let's start with the beginning. God created a perfect and harmonious world. He crafted a beautiful garden called Eden, where everything was in balance and harmony. God created Adam and Eve as image bearers, created in the image of God, *Imago Dei*. This garden was a place of perfect fellowship between God and humanity, a place where Adam and Eve, the first man and woman, could walk and talk with their Creator. God also entrusted them to rule and have authority over the Garden and all that He had created. The beauty and serenity of the garden were unrivaled, and all that God created was "good."

However, this idyllic existence was not to last. With the introduction of sin into the world through Adam and Eve's choice to eat from the tree of the knowledge of good and evil, the once-perfect creation was no longer the dwelling place for humanity. This knowledge of good and evil brought division out of misjudgment, and their choice to disobey God brought forth sin. Sin brought with it the consequences of suffering, pain, and death.

The fellowship between God and humanity was shattered, plunging the world into darkness. Let me pause here and clarify: this was not God throwing a tantrum because humans dared to eat from the forbidden tree. When Adam and Eve partook of it, God sought them out, but they chose to hide. They distanced themselves, prompting God to swiftly devise a rescue plan to restore communion with His sons and daughters. Sin entered the world, forcing Adam and Eve out of the garden, guarded by an angel wielding a flaming sword. God's aim was to prevent them from eating from the tree of life while in sin. Why? Because God desired for them to be redeemed back to His initial intent. Thus, life shifted from thriving in paradise to merely surviving. Humanity found itself confronting the harsh realities of mortality. The innocence of Eden was lost, and humanity grappled with existence outside God's original design. Adam's actions transitioned us from a garden to a grave. Yet, let's not forget: God's initial intent remains His final decision, and if it is not "good," then He is far from finished.

Here is a quick timeline of the events that occurred:

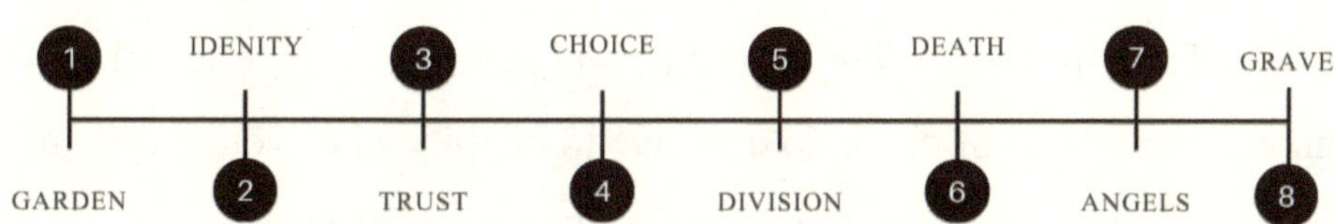

1. Garden: A paradise is created for humanity to dwell with God (Genesis 2:8-9).

2. Identity: Humanity is created in the image of God, *Imago Dei* (Genesis 1:26-27).

3. Trust: God trusts humanity by giving them responsibilities in the garden (Genesis 1:28-30).
4. Choice: Adam and Eve choose to eat from the forbidden tree (Genesis 2:16-17).
5. Division: Adam and Eve's choice brings division (Genesis 3:6).
6. Death: They are revoked from having access to the tree of life (Genesis 3:17-19).
7. Angels: God places cherubim to guard the way to the tree of life (Genesis 3:22-24).
8. Grave: Humanity digs a grave and needs a resurrection (Genesis 3:23-24).

Jesus has now begun to reverse this fall. If God's original intent is always going to be His final decision, what does that say about the reversal, and what does it say about the Garden? It means your story can begin and end in the Garden. He has provided a way back. The fall of man and the effects of death do not have to be the end of your story. In fact, there is much more to the story than you may realize.

Grave:

Let's fast forward to John chapter 20. Mary Magdalene arrives at Jesus' tomb or grave only to find the stone has been removed. She rushes to

Simon Peter and the other disciple (John), informing them that the Lord's body is missing. They visit the empty tomb, then return home, leaving Mary weeping outside. Then, something remarkable occurs.

In verse 13 of chapter 20 in the Gospel of John, angels approach Mary after the disciples depart. "Why are you crying?" they ask. "They have taken my Lord away," she replies, "and I don't know where they have put him." Turning around, she sees Jesus standing there, yet fails to recognize him. When He addresses her as "woman," she still does not realize it is him, mistaking him for the gardener in verse 15. She pleads, "Sir, if you have carried him away, tell me where you have put him, and I will get him." Then Jesus, calling her by name, says, "Mary." In response, she turns toward him, exclaiming in Aramaic, "*Rabbi.*"

Did you catch that? While at the tomb where Jesus lies, Mary experiences a moment where the story of Adam begins to unravel. Instead of seeing the man she knows and loves, she perceives a gardener. This revelation is profound.

Turning back to verse 41 of chapter 19, we learn that Jesus was crucified in a garden, where a new tomb stood. As Jesus emerges from the grave, He steps into a garden. Just as Adam left the garden and entered the grave, Jesus' plan is to reverse this cycle. He did not come merely to exist; He came to redeem. Jesus aims to overturn everything Adam set in motion, allowing us to once again enjoy the beauty of the garden. Adam led us from a garden to a grave, but Jesus has now led us from a grave to a garden.

Angels:

Angels played a pivotal role both in the removal of Adam and Eve from the Garden and in Jesus' resurrection. In Genesis, when Adam and Eve were removed, an angel of the Lord with a flaming sword was stationed to guard the entrance (Genesis 3:24). This symbolized the separation between humanity and the paradise they once enjoyed.

However, when Jesus rose from the dead, angels were present once more in the garden tomb. Their message echoed with profound significance: "Why do you look for the living among the dead? He is not here; he has risen!" (Luke 24:5-6, NIV). This declaration was not merely about Jesus' triumph over death; it signified the commencement of the great reversal. With Jesus' resurrection, death lost its power. Life once again became accessible to humanity. The angels proclaimed not just the resurrection of Jesus but also the restoration of hope and the promise of eternal life. They no longer protected us from the tree of life; instead, proclaimed that eternal life is accessible once again.

~~Death~~ Life:

The resurrection signifies the ultimate reversal of humanity's fall. Through Jesus' resurrection, God not only undoes the curse of sin but also restores our access to the Garden of Eden, symbolizing a return to the original state of divine communion. In this profound act, we regain the opportunity for an abundant life, reminiscent of the paradise that existed in the beginning. The resurrection is not merely a condemnation of death but a declaration of God's profound love for humanity and His desire to reconcile us to Himself. As stated in John 3:16, "For God so loved the world that he gave his one and only Son, that whoever believes in him shall not perish but have eternal life."

Again, I love movies. When my son, Kye, was younger, when he first came home from Korea and joined the family, one of the ways we learned to bond and overcome the language barrier was to watch movies together. I will never forget watching Kye's reaction as he looked at the screen and watched what would ultimately become some of his favorite animated films. He was more than a little frightened at first. Have you ever noticed that even in animated films, sometimes, because of the music that plays, we often have this feeling of wondering whether things will really work out in the end? Are the bad guys going to win?

After enough movies, Kye realized the bad guys never win. The same is true in the story of the Resurrection. For so long, Satan, the deceiver, thought he had won. He thought that through his subtle manipulation, he had caused man to completely deny God and lose all access to the Garden. Cue scary, sinister music. Everything changed, though, as Jesus made his triumphant exit from the empty tomb. As Jesus stepped out of the tomb, He stepped into a garden. And by doing so, He gave us a way back to the Garden as well.

~~Division~~ Unity:

The unity restored through the resurrection of Jesus signifies a profound reconciliation between humanity and God. As explored in earlier chapters, our division from God stemmed from the introduction of sin into the world, which severed the intimate relationship between humanity and its Creator. However, through Jesus' sacrificial death and triumphant resurrection, the rift caused by sin is bridged, and we are offered the opportunity to be united with God once again.

This unity is not merely an abstract concept but a transformative reality that invites us into a deeper communion with God. Just as Jesus forgave our sins and provided a pathway to reconciliation with God, we are challenged to extend that same forgiveness to others. As emphasized in previous discussions, forgiveness is not only a fundamental aspect of Christian faith but also a practical expression of our unity with God. In forgiving others, we mirror the divine forgiveness extended to us through Jesus' sacrifice, thereby embodying the unity we have with God.

Moreover, the restored unity with God also fosters unity among believers, as we are all adopted into the family of God through Jesus Christ. This familial bond transcends earthly divisions and unites us as brothers and sisters in Christ. As mentioned in earlier chapters, this unity among believers is essential for fulfilling our collective purpose as the body of Christ, working together to advance God's kingdom on earth.

Therefore, the restoration of unity through the resurrection of Jesus is not only an invitation to reconciliation with God but also a call to embody unity in our relationships with others. By extending forgiveness and embracing our identity as children of God, we participate in the redemptive work initiated by Jesus, bringing about unity and reconciliation in a world divided by sin.

Choice:

Jesus, through His sacrificial death and glorious resurrection, presents us with a pivotal choice. He offers us the opportunity to be forgiven of our sins and to once again access the abundant life promised in the Garden of Eden. This choice is both an invitation and a challenge, calling us to respond to God's grace and enter into the Kingdom of God.

Jesus' death on the cross was the ultimate payment for our sins, providing a way for reconciliation between humanity and God. His resurrection signifies victory over sin and death, demonstrating His power to bring new life to all who believe in Him. In essence, Jesus is not just a historical figure who was resurrected; He embodies resurrection itself, offering transformation and renewal to every aspect of our lives.

However, just like it was in the garden, this choice is not forced upon us; rather, it is a decision that each individual must make for themselves. Jesus extends His hand in invitation, but it is up to us to accept His offer of life.

Jesus declares Himself to be the only way to God, emphasizing the exclusivity of His message. This assertion echoes throughout Scripture, as Jesus proclaims, "I am the way and the truth and the life. No one comes to the Father except through me" (John 14:6). Thus, our choice to follow Jesus is not merely one among many options; it is the decisive path to eternal life and communion with God.

Trust:

After Jesus' resurrection, He began to appear to His disciples. In a post-resurrection conversation with Peter, Jesus probes the depths of love and commitment. Repeatedly, Jesus asks Peter, "Do you love me?" Through this questioning, Jesus not only reaffirms Peter's devotion but also commissions him to care for His followers. Each time Peter affirms his love for Jesus, he is given a specific charge: "Feed my lambs," "Take care of my sheep," and "Feed my sheep." These directives symbolize the profound responsibility entrusted to Peter and, by extension, to all believers.

This passage underscores the significance of the trust God has once again placed in our hands as sons and daughters of God. Just as Jesus entrusted Peter with the care of His followers, He entrusts us with the task of nurturing and guiding those around us. He trusts us with His creation. This trust is not to be taken lightly; it is a sacred responsibility that requires faithfulness and integrity.

Moreover, Jesus' unwavering confidence in Peter's love and commitment reflects His deep understanding of human nature. Despite Peter's past failures and shortcomings, Jesus sees beyond his flaws and recognizes the sincerity of his love. Similarly, Jesus sees into the depths of our hearts and calls us to follow Him with wholehearted devotion.

By entrusting us with the care of His flock, Jesus invites us to participate in His redemptive work in the world. We are called to feed His lambs, tend His sheep, and nurture His followers, bringing out the redemptive qualities of the world around us. In doing so, we demonstrate our love for Jesus and fulfill our role as faithful stewards of His kingdom.

Identity:

Our identity as believers has been fully reestablished through our relationship with Christ. Through His sacrificial death and resurrection, we are no longer estranged from God but are welcomed into His family as beloved children. The apostle Paul writes in Romans 8:15-17:
"The Spirit you received does not make you slaves, so that you live in

fear again; rather, the Spirit you received brought about your adoption to sonship. And by Him we cry, 'Abba, Father.' The Spirit Himself testifies with our spirit that we are God's children. Now, if we are children, then we are heirs. We are heirs of God and co-heirs with Christ, if indeed we share in His sufferings in order that we may also share in His glory."

Through the redemptive work of Jesus Christ, we are adopted into God's family and granted the privilege of calling Him "Abba, Father." This adoption carries with it an inheritance as heirs of God's kingdom, sharing in the glory of Christ Himself.

Moreover, our identity is defined by the covering of Jesus' blood, which cleanses us from sin and restores us to our original state of goodness in God's eyes. Just as God declared His creation "good" in the beginning (Genesis 1:31), He affirms our inherent worth and value through the atoning sacrifice of His Son. As recipients of God's grace, we are seen as righteous and blameless in His sight, clothed in the righteousness of Christ. We are once again seen as Imago Dei, the image of God.

This understanding of identity empowers us to live with confidence and purpose, knowing that we are deeply loved and accepted by our Heavenly Father. It shapes how we view ourselves and others, leading us to extend grace and compassion to those around us. As children of God, we are called to reflect His image and bring glory to His name in all that we do.

Garden:

The great reversal brings us to a profound realization: we are no longer passive observers of God's restoration work but active participants in His ongoing redemption story. We must stop viewing the garden from a distance and instead begin participating in it. Through the resurrection of Jesus Christ, the Garden of fellowship and intimacy with God is once again open to us. We are invited not merely to gaze upon it from a distance but to step into its midst and experience its beauty and abundance firsthand.

We are called to engage fully in the work of cultivating and nurturing the Garden of God's kingdom here on earth. This means living out our faith with authenticity and purpose, extending love and grace to those around us, and actively seeking to bring healing and restoration to a broken world, on earth as it is in Heaven.

The Room with the Garden View resonates deeply within our hearts, reminding us that our ultimate longing is for intimacy with our Creator. Yet too often, we settle for a mere glimpse of the Garden from a comfortable distance, content to remain in the safety of our familiar surroundings. But Jesus beckons us to more. He invites us to step out of our comfort zones, to embrace the adventure of faith, and to walk alongside Him in the fullness of life that He offers. He is not a distant figure waiting for us in some far-off land; rather, He is here with us, longing to walk beside us each and every day.

I implore you to embrace the abundant life that Jesus offers. Let us no longer settle for a room with a Garden view; instead, let us fully enter into the beauty and wonder of the Garden itself. In doing so, we will experience the joy of true fellowship with God that Jesus died to give.

Chapter 9: The Path Back to the Garden

As humans, we often make poor decisions for ourselves, especially when it comes to our relationship with God. We're so conditioned to think that our way is better, but where has that really gotten us? It's time to realize that God has something much better in store for us than we could ever imagine. But in order to receive what God has for us, we must believe that He has a better offer than what we are currently settling for. To to do that, we need a complete change of heart and mind. When we settle for what we have for so long, we begin to think it is truly the best. However, in the Garden, there's always more. And it's always better.

Countless stories in the Bible show how people settled for less than what God wanted for them, from the Fall of Man in the Garden of Eden to the earthly life and ministry of Jesus. Even John the Baptist, who paved the way for Jesus' message, preached the word "Repent." The Greek word for "repent" is "*metanoia,*" which means to change your mind. John was saying that to receive the coming Messiah, you had to change the way you think of Him. *You can never receive what you do not first perceive.*

Perception matters a lot. For too long, we've viewed ourselves and God incorrectly, preventing us from realizing that God's ways are much better than ours. People missed who Jesus was because they had predetermined ideas of what the Messiah would look like. We can relate to that as well. How often have we remained distant from God because of our own preconceived notions and ideas about Him?

Satan loves it when we are unwilling to change our minds because he wins every time. Jesus said, "Repent, for the kingdom of heaven has come near." But unless we change our minds, we will miss it. God has made a way for His initial intent to become His final decision, but we must first change the way we think. We must put on the mind of Christ.

In today's world, we think that just by thinking positively, we can have all the changes our hearts desire. But most of the time, it never works out the way we think or expect. We end up getting ourselves into even more trouble. It seems we've come to think that success means doing things on our own, but that's simply more death. To change the way we think, we need to have our minds renewed and have the mind of Christ dwelling in us.

Sometimes, we think that God is out to steal our fun or freedom, but that couldn't be further from the truth. We settle for a room with a view of the garden instead of taking Jesus' invitation to come to the Garden. We forget that all the burdens and struggles we allow in our lives were never part of God's original plan for us. He wants to bear our burdens and give us an even greater life, eternal life.

Again, believing a partial truth is simply embracing a believable lie. We've settled for a feeling of control in the moment, thinking that we're in charge. But all the while, we're just taking on the wages of sin, which is always death. There's always more to the story, and because of what Jesus did, we can actually have a different ending to our story. Life can be much, much different than what it is now.

In the grand tapestry of life, there is always a greater narrative at play. It's not just about the here and now; there's more to the story. Because of the profound reversal Jesus accomplished, your story can have a different ending. Life can be radically transformed from what it is today.

Consider the intricate dynamics of a chess game. Consider the strategic moves, the calculated maneuvers. It all culminates in a pivotal moment when the kings, unable to make another move, face their ultimate fate. In the illustrious halls of the Louvre Museum, an extraordinary painting hangs, titled *Checkmate,* a masterpiece by Friedrich Moritz August Retzsch. This captivating artwork portrays two chess players locked in a fierce battle. One player, Satan himself, exudes arrogance, his confidence suggesting an imminent victory. The other player, burdened and weary, appears to anticipate defeat, overwhelmed by the seemingly inevitable outcome.

Yet, amid this intense confrontation, a profound revelation emerges. There is a story, often told, of a chess grandmaster, drawn to the painting's magnetic allure, who stood before it in awe. His gaze fixated on the intricacies of the chessboard depicted, his mind engaged in a dance with the artistry before him. And in that moment, he discovered something astounding. Despite Satan's apparent advantage, a hidden truth unveiled itself… the player who appeared to be losing could still win. His king had another move.

This captivating tale mirrors the story of our lives. We find ourselves engaged in a battle, grappling with challenges and adversity, as Satan cunningly lures us towards defeat. But take heart, for the grandmaster's revelation holds a powerful message for us. In the spiritual realm, the tables can be turned. What appears to be a guaranteed loss can transform into an astounding triumph. Through the great reversal brought about by Jesus, victory is within reach.

The parallel between the chessboard and our lives is profound. Satan may exude confidence, his tactics seemingly foolproof, but the truth remains that he is about to be overcome. *The King always has another move*

As we navigate the complexities of life, let us be reminded that the apparent victor is not always the ultimate conqueror. In Christ, we possess the key to victory. We have the power to unleash a fateful move that will reshape the course of our lives and defy the expectations of the enemy. Just as the grandmaster's revelation sparked a paradigm shift, may our understanding of this truth ignite a fire within us, propelling us towards the abundant life God has ordained for us.

So, my friend, do not be deceived by the temporary victories of the enemy. Stop settling for a view of the garden as your guide to the life God has for you. Accept the invitation to return to the garden, to embrace God's initial intent for your existence. This is not a journey you have to undertake without guidance. The Word of God, with its timeless wisdom and profound insights, will serve as a radiant light, illuminating your path back home.

Just as the grandmaster's move determined the outcome of the chess game, your move, in alignment with God's divine plan, will determine the trajectory of your life. You have been strategically positioned for victory, armed with the instructions and direction necessary to overcome every obstacle. Embrace the fullness of what God has in store for you, for His initial intent is His final decision. Forgiveness is God's grace extended to you in order that God can continue to move through you.

Forgiveness is the solution for sin, and it is what paves the road from the grave to the Garden. Repentance is simply following the path home to the Garden. And that path begins with a change of mind. Repentance is not just about confessing and turning away from sin; it is also about changing our perspective, our worldview, and our understanding of God's ways.

As we have discussed throughout this book, the Garden represents God's initial intent for humanity. It is a place of communion with God, where we can experience His love, joy, peace, and purpose. It is a place where we can find rest for our souls and fulfillment for our deepest longings. But we lost access to the Garden because of sin. We were separated from God and from His initial intent for our lives. We were left wandering in the wilderness, searching for something that could satisfy the longing in our hearts.

But God did not abandon us. He had a plan to bring us back to the Garden, to restore us to His initial intent. And that plan involved the person of Jesus Christ. The King always had another move. Through His life, death, and resurrection, Jesus made a way for us to be forgiven of our sin and to be reconciled to God. He opened the door to the Garden and invited us to come in.

But in order to enter the Garden, we must first repent. We must change our minds about sin and about God's ways. We must realize that the path we have been walking on is not leading us to the Garden, but rather to a dead-end. We must recognize that there is a better way, a way that leads to life and not to death. We must turn away from our old way of thinking and embrace a new way of thinking, the mind of Christ.

What does it mean to have the mind of Christ? It means viewing ourselves, others, and the world around us through the lens of God's initial intent. It means seeing ourselves as loved, valued, and created by God, and seeing others in the same way. It means to see the world as a place of beauty and wonder, created by a loving God who desires our flourishing. It means to see sin as a barrier to experiencing God's love.

But how do we cultivate the mind of Christ? How do we change our minds to align with God's initial intent? The answer lies in renewing our minds through the power of the Holy Spirit and the Word of God. Romans 12:2 says, *"Do not be conformed to this world, but be transformed by the renewal of your mind, that by testing you may discern what is the will of God, what is good and acceptable and perfect."*

Renewing our minds is a lifelong process that requires discipline, intentionality, and perseverance. It involves reading, studying, and meditating on the Word of God, and allowing it to shape our thoughts, attitudes, and behaviors. It involves prayer and seeking the guidance of the Holy Spirit, who empowers us to think and act in ways that are pleasing to God. It involves community and fellowship with other believers, who can encourage us, challenge us, and hold us accountable on our journey.

This transformation is not just for our personal benefit, but for the sake of the Kingdom of God. As we align ourselves with God's will and participate in His mission, we become agents of change in the world around us. We become a living testimony to the transformative power of the Gospel.

It's important to note that the path back to the Garden is not a solo journey. We need the support and accountability of a community of believers to walk alongside us and encourage us. As Proverbs 27:17 states, *"As iron sharpens iron, so one person sharpens another." In community, we can be vulnerable and honest about our struggles and receive the support and guidance we need to continue on the path of transformation."*

Transformation is what our soul longs for. Throughout our lives, we have been inundated with a dangerous lie, one that whispers in our ears, enticing us to believe that the "good life" is found solely in our own efforts and accomplishments. But is this truly the essence of a fulfilled existence? Is it possible that we have been deceived by the enemy, cunningly led astray from the path of dependence on God and the transformative journey of repentance?

Consider for a moment the prevailing narrative that promotes self-reliance and individualistic pursuits as the gateway to the "good life." It permeates our culture, subtly ingraining in our minds the notion that true success and happiness can be achieved through our own merit. But let us pause and reflect on the implications of this ideology.

According to 2020 CDC data, 63% of 18-24-year-olds reported symptoms of anxiety and depression. 25% reported increased substance abuse in order to find a way out. Another 25% said they have seriously considered suicide. And this is what we call the "good life"? The reality is that there's always more than meets the eye. Is God really trying to take away your good life, or is He instead trying to give you an even greater life? Sometimes when we think about the good life, we think about the good life of fun, freedom, and having things on our own. But is this life really all that good? I mean, is it really?

The truth is, the so-called "good life" is not found in our own isolated endeavors. It is not a product of our self-reliance or self-made achievements. True fulfillment, abundance, and purpose are discovered in the intimate relationship we cultivate with God, the source of all goodness and grace.

In the Garden of Eden, Adam and Eve were tempted by the enemy's insidious lie that they could be like God, independent and self-sufficient. The consequences of that deception reverberate through the ages, as humanity continues to grapple with the consequences of our longing for autonomy. Yet, amid our waywardness, God beckons us back to Himself, offering a path of repentance as the gateway to restoration and true fulfillment.

We need to be willing to let go of our preconceived notions and embrace God's initial intent for our lives. This requires a change of mind, a turning away from the things that lead us astray and a turning towards God and His ways. As we align ourselves with God's will and participate in His mission, we can experience the fullness of life that He intended for us from the beginning.

Our own minds can also deceive us into thinking that we have everything under control, that we have all the answers, and that we know what is best for our lives. This is a dangerous and prideful mindset that can lead us down a path of destruction. Proverbs 14:12 states, "There is a way that appears to be right, but in the end, it leads to death." When we trust in our own understanding and our own ways, we are ultimately rejecting God's plan and His wisdom for our lives. To truly experience the abundant life God has for us, we must submit to His will and trust in His guidance.

As we journey back to the Garden, we must also recognize the importance of forgiveness in our lives. Sin is a barrier that separates us from God, but through the sacrifice of Jesus Christ, we have been granted forgiveness and reconciliation with God. We must also extend this same forgiveness to others in our lives, as Matthew 6:14-15 states, *"For if you forgive other people when they sin against you, your heavenly Father will also forgive you. But if you do not forgive others their sins, your Father will not forgive your sins."* Forgiveness is not just an act of obedience to God, but it also frees us from the burden of bitterness and resentment that can poison our souls."

A few months back, I gave Kye a new Lego set. I remember sitting and watching him open up his brand new Lego set, and excitement swelled within him. The 700-piece set was a dinosaur, and he couldn't wait to get started building it. But as he opened up the box, his face quickly changed from pure joy to utter disappointment. The instructions were nowhere to be found. As I frantically searched for them, Kye sat there with a look of uncertainty on his face. How was he supposed to build this without the instructions?

But then, something amazing happened. Kye looked at the picture on the front of the box, and he had an idea. "It's okay, papa," he said with determination. "I can just build it from looking at the finished dinosaur on the outside of the box." And with that, he began to build.

Though he was frustrated at times, Kye never gave up. He used his creativity and his own understanding of how things fit together to build something truly amazing. Kye continued to work diligently on his dinosaur, occasionally stopping to examine the picture on the box. As he worked, he would mutter to himself about how he wished he had the instructions. I watched him struggle, amazed by his determination and persistence. Finally, after what seemed like hours, he proudly held up his creation for me to see. "It's not perfect," he said, "but I did it!" I was impressed with his ability to build the dinosaur without the instructions. But then he looked at me and said, "Imagine what it would have looked like if I had the directions."

His words struck a chord with me. How often do we try to navigate life without following the instructions God has given us? How many times have we settled for a life that is less than what God intended for us, simply because we didn't take the time to seek His direction? Just like Kye with his dinosaur, we may be able to build something on our own, but it will never be as good as it could have been if we had followed the instructions. How often do we try to create something without following the proper instructions? How often do we rely on our own understanding and creativity to build something that's supposed to be beautiful and meaningful, only to end up with a creation that falls short?

But just like Kye tried to build from the picture on the box, we too take a partial image of God and try to create a "Christian life" that resembles it. The good news is we have access to the instructions for building a life of meaning and purpose. God has given us the Bible as our guide and Jesus as our example. Through His death and resurrection, He has made a path for us to experience the fullness of life that He intended for us. This path is repentance.

I am proud of what you have accomplished on your own efforts in your attempt to create a faith by observing God in your life. But just like Kye's dinosaur, I believe that there is something even more amazing waiting for us if we use the proper instructions. With God's guidance, we can build a life that exceeds our wildest dreams, a life that truly reflects His love and grace.

Don't settle for a distant view of the garden as your guide to the life God has in store for you. Instead, accept His invitation to journey back to the Garden, and be reminded that you don't have to navigate this path without direction. Let the Word of God be a light that illuminates your path and guides you back to the Garden, where you can experience the fullness of God's original intent for your life.

The path back to the Garden requires a willingness to change our minds and align ourselves with God's ways. It's a journey of repentance and transformation that requires the support and accountability of a community of believers. As we surrender control to God and participate in His mission, we become agents of change in the world around us, living testimonies to the transformative power of the Gospel. Now we can not only experience the Garden also show the way!

Chapter 10: Tending the Garden

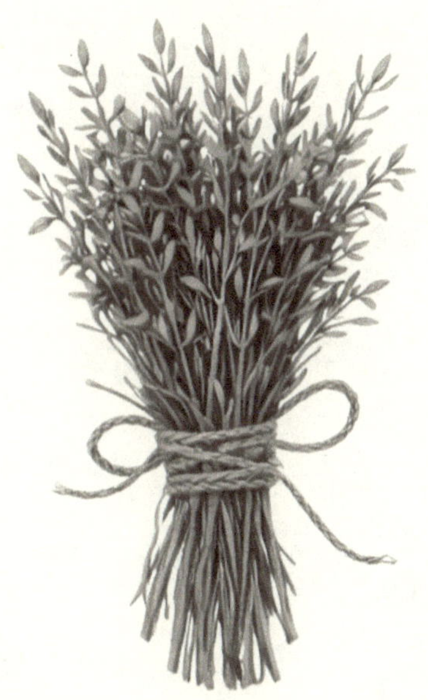

Have you ever felt as if God's promises were distant, beyond your reach? Life's challenges, our own missteps, and the distractions of this world can often obscure our vision and make it difficult to fully trust in God. In those moments, we might wonder if He genuinely has our best interests at heart. But let me assure you, there is profound beauty and reliability in God's promises. They are not hollow words; when God makes a promise, He always provides a provision. If God has made a promise, rest assured, He will provide everything needed to fulfill it.

Throughout my years as a pastor and minister, a recurring question has arisen: Is a life of faith truly worth it? Is it worthwhile to trust in God and wholeheartedly follow Christ? As we've explored in the preceding chapters, the resounding answer is: "Yes." God isn't interested in curtailing our freedom; rather, He seeks to offer us something far greater. He yearns to bestow upon us the life we've always dreamed of, a life that can only be discovered in Him. God isn't intent on restricting our enjoyment of life's blessings; on the contrary, He desires to provide an even more abundant life than we can envision.

What if I were to tell you that Jesus not only made it possible for you to find your way back to the Garden but also supplied a provision that empowers you to dwell in the Garden? A provision that grants you authentic staying power, ensuring you never have to leave the Garden again. This provision bestows upon you the strength and capacity to break free from the cycle of repeated mistakes. Such a claim may seem astonishing, but let me elaborate.

In this life, you are not alone. As a believer, you've been granted the promise of genuine staying power. It's the power that enables you to fulfill every God-given calling in your life. However, we often wrestle with fully embracing these promises. Doubt and uncertainty can creep in, causing us to question whether God's promises are genuinely intended for us. But today, I implore you to wholeheartedly embrace the promises of God, for He is faithful and true to His Word.

Let me share a personal story that underscores the significance of faith and belief. Several years ago, my family and I embarked on a vacation to a picturesque lake. The scenery was breathtaking, with crystal-clear waters and lush foliage enveloping us. It was a much-needed escape, a time to unwind and rejuvenate.

During our vacation, I decided to take my daughter, Wendy, fishing. We ventured to the marina store to purchase some bait, worms to be specific. Now, I confess that I knew little about fishing worms, so when the woman behind the counter inquired about the type of worms we desired, I was taken aback. She listed various options, but what caught my attention was "Alabama jumping worms."

Intrigued by the notion of using such lively, active worms for fishing, I decided to give them a try. We bought a container of these Alabama jumping worms and returned to our campsite.

Late that night, my wife, Cassie, awakened and accidentally stepped on something soft and squishy. Confused and still half-asleep, she quickly grabbed a flashlight to investigate. To our amazement, the entire floor of our camper was covered in worms, Alabama jumping worms, precisely as the lady from the marina store had described. It was a sight to behold, and we couldn't help but marvel at how these worms genuinely lived up to their reputation.

I share this story to illustrate how often we are told something but struggle to believe it until we see it with our own eyes. We may hear the promises of God, yet doubt lingers in our hearts. We find it difficult to accept that God can genuinely provide a way for us, that His promises are not mere empty words. But I want to assure you that with every promise God makes, He always provides the provision to bring it to pass. When God speaks, His words are not mere wishes or hopes; they are unwavering assurances.

Consider the words of Jesus in Acts 1:8: "But you will receive power when the Holy Spirit comes upon you, and you will be my witnesses in Jerusalem, and in all Judea and Samaria, and to the ends of the earth." These words convey the promise of power, the power of the Holy Spirit that empowers us to be effective witnesses for Christ. God longs to fill you so that you can fulfill the purpose He has designed for your life.

The fulfillment of this promise is vividly depicted in Acts 2:1-8, where the disciples experienced the outpouring of the Holy Spirit on the day of Pentecost. As they gathered together in one place, a sound like a violent wind filled the house, and they saw what appeared to be tongues of fire resting upon each of them. They were filled with the Holy Spirit and began to speak in other tongues as the Spirit enabled them. This miraculous event astounded those who witnessed it, as people from different nations heard the disciples speaking in their native languages.

The promises of God are never given without a purpose. Each promise carries a divine intention. You, my friend, have been summoned to accomplish remarkable deeds in the Kingdom of God. You've been chosen not only to live an extraordinary and remarkable life but also to share the glory of God with others. Now that you've been restored to the Garden, you are commissioned to invite others into this beautiful and abundant life.

God has placed a unique mission before us, and He will supply all the necessary resources to accomplish it. He didn't ask us to succeed in our own strength; rather, He called us to be faithful. When we contemplate the enormity of God's call, it can feel overwhelming at times. Thoughts such as "I can't do that" or "Who would listen to me?" may arise within us. We may doubt our ability to make a difference or question the value of our contribution. But let me assure you that God is able to provide everything you need to fulfill His call.

It is time to transition from being mere observers of the Garden to walking intimately with God once again. We must trade our rooms with a garden view for active roles as contributors, not just consumers. It is not enough to taste and see that God is good; we must also reveal the flavors of the Garden to the world around us. It is our responsibility to tell others about the beauty and abundance found in a life lived in close relationship with God.

Jesus affirmed that the Kingdom of God is not confined to a specific location; it is in our midst. As believers who have experienced the Kingdom, our role is to tend the garden, to steward the fruit of the Garden, and display the Kingdom of God through the work of the Holy Spirit. Our lives become a living testimony, an invitation for others to encounter the transformative power of God.

In 1 Corinthians 3:6-9, the apostle Paul beautifully illustrates the collaborative nature of our work in God's service: "I planted the seed, Apollos watered it, but God has been making it grow. So neither the one who plants nor the one who waters is anything, but only God, who makes things grow. The one who plants and the one who waters have one purpose, and they will each be rewarded according to their own labor. For we are co-workers in God's service; you are God's field, God's building."

This passage emphasizes that we are not alone in this task. We may play different roles, some sowing the seed and others watering it, but ultimately it is God who brings growth and transformation. Our labor is not in vain when it is aligned with God's purposes.

Remember the shocking and tragic statistics we discussed earlier in the book? They represent real people, individuals who are still trying to navigate through life, just like you. They are people who are merely surviving rather than thriving. Isn't it time for them to experience the beauty of the Garden as well?

We have been entrusted with a message of hope, a message that can transform lives and bring restoration. It is our privilege and responsibility to share this message with others. As we tend the garden of our own lives, we have the opportunity to impact those around us. Our lives can become a living testimony, a visible demonstration of the goodness and faithfulness of God.

In conclusion, the promises of God are not distant or unattainable. They are real, and they carry with them the assurance of provision. God will always make a way for His promises to come to pass. His initial intent is His final decision. Therefore, when God speaks, we can trust in His faithfulness and confidently believe that every promise He has made will be fulfilled.

As we walk in faith, we experience the power of the Holy Spirit at work in our lives. We are empowered to fulfill our God-given purpose and make a significant impact in the world. It is time to embrace our role as stewards of the Garden, to tend the fruit and to display the Kingdom of God through our lives.

Let us not be held back by doubt or fear but instead step boldly into the calling that God has placed upon us. Together, as co-workers in God's service, let us faithfully tend the Garden, inviting others to experience the beauty, abundance, and transformative power of a life lived in close relationship with God.

And as we fulfill our purpose, let us remember the words of 1 Corinthians 3:9: "For we are co-workers in God's service; you are God's field, God's building." We are not alone in this journey. God is with us, equipping us, and empowering us to make a lasting impact in His Kingdom.

May the Garden flourish, and may the world be transformed as we faithfully tend to God's Kingdom.

Chapter 11: A Day in the Garden

As I mentioned at the beginning of this book, when we don't know the truth for ourselves, any story can become our narrative. Satan loves nothing more than to cause us to buy into half-truths. This is one of his many tricks. With this, he deceives us and manipulates us into believing that we should settle for the lives we have. He would love nothing more than for us to settle for the fallen state. He casually omits the part about the resurrection, bringing about the great reversal. So, as a result, sometimes we just think this is all there is. Surely God doesn't have anything better for us.

Genesis 2:1-3 states, *"Thus the heavens and the earth were completed in all their vast array. By the seventh day God had finished the work he had been doing; so on the seventh day he rested from all his work. Then God blessed the seventh day and made it holy, because on it he rested from all the work of creating that he had done."*

But for a moment, let's go back to the beginning again. When God formed Adam and Eve and placed them in the beautiful and perfect Garden, He instructed them not to eat of the Tree of the Knowledge of Good and Evil. But as we know by now, this wasn't because God was trying to steal all of their fun or take away their joy. It wasn't because He was trying to deprive them of the good life. In fact, surprisingly, it wasn't even that God didn't want Adam and Eve to eat. No, far from it. The real issue, you see, was that God wanted Adam and Eve to be able to eat forever.

In life, we're always eating something. We're always consuming something. Most often, though, we're just consuming things that never truly satisfy. Remember the story of the woman at the well? Jesus said to her, "I've got something that's going to truly satisfy you." Think of that. Imagine that. Something that truly satisfies our souls, something that we can enjoy forever. Well, my friend, this is what life in the Garden truly looks like. It looks like truly being satisfied.

The rhythms of a day in the Garden, the patterns of life in the Kingdom, are what Jesus came to reveal and invite us into. Jesus died so that we could live forever, but He lived to reveal the Kingdom rhythms we are called to step into each and every day.

Jesus extends an invitation to walk with Him, a call that often feels risky. It may seem risky to walk with Jesus. But it is far riskier to walk without Jesus. As we journey through life, the steps we take matter. "You have to take steps in order to walk, but you're not always walking just because you took a step." Steps lead to walking, and walking with God is what we long for you to experience.

But sometimes, even when we are in the right place and the right time, we are facing the wrong direction. Recently, our golden doodle, Toby, reminded me of this truth. Toby joined our family as a rambunctious puppy, wild, crazy, and perfectly suited to the chaos of our household. When we hired a trainer to help guide Toby's energy, the trainer emphasized a principle that stuck with me: to keep Toby moving in the right direction, sometimes you have to make an abrupt turn. A quick change in direction forces him to reevaluate not just his location but also his orientation. This forces him to refocus and align with the path we are walking.

This principle mirrors our own journey with God. How often have we felt like life would be better if only we had a new job, a different spouse, easier kids, more money, or lived in another place? Satan convinces us that we need something different. But the truth is, you may be in the right place, at the right time, with all the resources you need. You're just facing the wrong direction.

God is more concerned with our orientation than our location. Throughout the Gospels, we see that proximity to Jesus does not always equate to alignment with Him. The Pharisees and Sadducees stood physically closer to Jesus than most, attending synagogues and observing the law with scrupulous care. By all appearances, their location placed them near God. Yet their hearts were oriented away from Him. Their steps, though precise in outward appearance, led them further from God because they resisted the truth of who Jesus was. Their pride and self-righteousness blinded them to the very Messiah they awaited.

Contrast this with the woman at the well. By every cultural and religious standard of the day, she was far from God. A Samaritan, a woman, and someone whose life bore the scars of sin and rejection, she was as much an outsider as one could be. Yet her orientation was turned toward Jesus. In her conversation with Him, she sought truth and responded with faith. While the Pharisees' steps led them away, her steps, despite her location, brought her closer to God. This encounter reveals a profound truth: it is not where you stand but which way you are facing that matters to God.

We also see this pattern in Zacchaeus, the tax collector. Though despised and excluded by his community, Zacchaeus climbed a tree just to catch a glimpse of Jesus. His physical distance was great, but his heart leaned toward the Savior. Jesus called him down, dined at his house, and declared, "Today salvation has come to this house" (Luke 19:9). Augustine of Hippo observed, “God is always trying to give good things to us, but our hands are too full to receive them.” The Pharisees’ hands were full of their own self-righteousness, while Zacchaeus and the woman at the well approached Jesus empty-handed, ready to receive His grace.

This truth reminds us that we can never be too far for God to reach us if we are turned toward Him. Like the Samaritan woman and Zacchaeus, orientation matters more than location. As Origen wrote, "The soul that looks towards God has been instructed to keep its face towards Him at all times." God calls us to turn our hearts to Him, to face Jesus, and to take steps toward Him, no matter how far we feel we have wandered. For even a small step in the right direction is enough to draw us closer to the Gardener who seeks to walk with us in the garden once again.

In this Garden, we find the fruit of the Spirit flourishing in abundance: love, joy, peace, patience, kindness, goodness, faithfulness, gentleness, and self-control. This fruit is evidence of a day in the garden. God offers this fruit as a result of communing with Him, but where this fruit is absent, the world tries to offer us substitutes. Where there is a lack of fruit, we will begin to substitute in with artificial flavors that mimic what only the Spirit can truly provide. The world will try to give you a substitute, but it will never satisfy.

Think about artificial flavors. They may resemble the fruit they are imitating, but they often leave a bitter aftertaste or fail to satisfy our cravings. As believers, we need to know that our lives are to be an invitation for the world to "taste and see," but they can smell artificial from a mile away. We wonder why people seem to have such a bad taste in their mouths when it comes to God and Christianity. Maybe because we have settled for artificial flavors instead of the fruit that comes from abiding in God and God alone. The world offers us fleeting pleasures that only leave us more empty: false joy in material wealth, artificial peace in fleeting distractions, and shallow connections masquerading as love. These substitutes may seem appealing, but they cannot fill the deep longing of our hearts for the real fruit that only God can produce.

A day in the Garden is one that has chosen to surrender our ways to God. At this point, I pray you have embraced the truth that you will never enjoy God's presence apart from His guidance. In the Garden,

Adam and Eve walked with God, enjoying uninterrupted communion with Him. But their disobedience severed this connection, replacing peace with shame. Walking with God requires submission to His guidance. It means allowing Him to lead, trusting that His ways are higher than ours. It is in surrendering to His direction that we rediscover the joy of His presence. There is more.

The invitation to the Garden is an invitation to not settle for the lies of this world but to experience more of God and the things of God. The Kingdom is not some far-off promise; it is among us. Luke 17:21 reminds us, *"Nor will they say, 'See here!' or 'See there!' For indeed, the kingdom of God is within you."*

The truth is, every one of us is as close to God as we choose to be. The choice to walk with Him is ours. He is not distant or unreachable. Instead, He calls us to step into His rhythms of grace, to align our lives with His Kingdom, and to live in His presence each day. A day in the Garden reflects a life lived in the fullness of God's design. It means walking closely with Jesus, allowing Him to direct our paths, and embracing the rhythms of grace that bring peace and joy. It is a life of purpose, where every step we take is aligned with the Gardener who walks beside us.

And while walking with Jesus may feel risky, remember: "It may seem risky to walk with Jesus. But it is far riskier to walk without Jesus." My deepest prayer, my heart's cry, is that we would all walk so closely with Jesus here on Earth that the line between this life and eternity becomes almost imperceptible. Imagine living with such intimacy, such faithfulness, that when the moment comes to take our last breath here, it is not a fearful leap into the unknown, but a gentle step into the continuation of a journey already begun. That as our eyes close in this life, they open in the presence of Jesus, and He meets us not as a stranger, but as the dearest companion of our soul. And in that sacred moment, He smiles, extends His hand, and simply says, "Where did we leave off?"

Think about that. No awkward reintroductions. No fumbling to explain why we drifted away. No regret for time wasted chasing after things that could never satisfy. Just the sweet familiarity of a relationship that has been nurtured, cultivated, and cherished daily. To walk with Jesus so closely that the veil between Earth and Heaven is but the thinnest of threads, a transition rather than a destination.

But, my friend, this is not automatic. It is not a result of merely believing or knowing about Him. This kind of relationship comes only through choosing, every day, to walk with Him. To turn our hearts toward Him, no matter how far we feel we've wandered. To step back onto the path when we've stumbled. To let Him lead us when we've lost our way. Every one of us is as close to God as we choose to be.

What will your choice be? Will you allow the noise of this world to drown out His voice, or will you tune your ears to hear His unforced rhythms of grace? Will you settle for the substitutes this world offers, or will you hunger for the fruit of the Spirit that only He can provide? Will you take a step today, a step that leads to walking, and walking that leads to intimacy with the Savior who longs to walk beside you?

The Garden is not just a place. It's an invitation. An invitation to not settle for the lies of this world, but to experience more of God, more of His presence, more of His love. It is a call to walk with Him now so that when the time comes to walk into eternity, it feels like the natural next step. My prayer for you, for me, for all of us, is that we will hear those beautiful, life-affirming words when that day comes: "Where did we leave off?"

As we conclude this journey, I invite you to step into the Garden.

Accept the invitation to walk with God, experience His presence, and live in the fullness of His Kingdom. The Kingdom is among us, and it is calling you to take the next step. May you find joy, peace, and purpose in the Garden. May you experience the abundant life that Jesus came to give. And may you always remember that you are loved beyond measure by the Gardener who walks with you every step of the way.

Notes and Citations

Augustine of Hippo. Sermons. Quoted in various collections of Augustine's sayings. The quotation, "God is always trying to give good things to us, but our hands are too full to receive them," is commonly attributed to Augustine.

Bible Hub. "Greek 3341. Metanoia." Bible Hub. Accessed May 2026. https://biblehub.com/greek/3341.htm.

Czeisler, Mark É., Rashon I. Lane, Emiko Petrosky, Joshua F. Wiley, Aleta Christensen, Rashid Njai, Matthew D. Weaver, Rebecca Robbins, Elise R. Facer-Childs, Laura K. Barger, Charles A. Czeisler, Mark E. Howard, and Shantha M. W. Rajaratnam. "Mental Health, Substance Use, and Suicidal Ideation During the COVID-19 Pandemic, United States, June 24-30, 2020." Morbidity and Mortality Weekly Report 69, no. 32. Centers for Disease Control and Prevention, August 14, 2020. https://doi.org/10.15585/mmwr.mm6932a1.

Family Times. "Bribed to Open the Gate of the Great Wall." Family Times. Accessed May 2026. https://www.family-times.net/commentary/the-renewal-of-israel-ezekiel-36-16/bribed-to-open-the-gate-of-the-great-wall-11809.

Kavanaugh, John F., S.J. "Godforsakenness: Finding One's Heart's Desire." America Magazine, October 1, 2007. https://www.americamagazine.org/columns/2007/10/01/godforsakenness.

Martin, James, S.J. "What You Can Learn About Doubt from Mother Teresa." Crosswalk, August 15, 2017. https://www.crosswalk.com/faith/spiritual-life/what-you-can-learn-about-doubt-from-mother-teresa.html.

Maxwell, John C. The Leader Within You. Nashville: Thomas Nelson, 1993.

"One More Move: Paul Morphy and the Moritz Retzsch Painting." One More Move Chess Art. Accessed May 2026. https://www.one-more-move-chess-art.com/One-More-Move.html.

Origen. On Prayer. Translated by William A. Curtis. In The Ante-Nicene Fathers, vol. 4, edited by Alexander Roberts, James Donaldson, and A. Cleveland Coxe. Buffalo, NY: Christian Literature Publishing Co., 1885. Revised and edited for New Advent by Kevin Knight. https://www.newadvent.org/fathers/0416.htm.

Retzsch, Friedrich Moritz August. Die Schachspieler [The Chess Players], commonly known as Checkmate, c. 1830s.

Social Security Administration. "Background Information for Popular Names." Social Security Administration. Accessed May 2026. https://www.ssa.gov/oact/babynames/background.html.

Social Security Administration. "Popular Baby Names: Beyond the Top 1000 Names." Social Security Administration. Accessed May 2026. https://www.ssa.gov/oact/babynames/limits.html.

www.ingramcontent.com/pod-product-compliance
Lightning Source LLC
La Vergne TN
LVHW091316150826
845673LV00006B/1662

979899595620 4